A WILD FLOWER

by any other

NAME

*Sketches of pioneer naturalists
who named our western plants*

KAREN B. NILSSON

YOSEMITE
ASSOCIATION

Copyright © 1994, Nils Nilsson
Art Copyright © 1994, Andrea Hendrick

Designed and illustrated by Andrea Hendrick

Edited by Diane Hart

Yosemite Association
P.O. Box 545
Yosemite National Park, CA 95389
(209) 379-2646

Library of Congress Cataloging-in-Publication Data

Nilsson, Karen B., 1936-1991.
    A wild flower by any other name: sketches of pioneer
naturalists who named our western plants / by Karen B.
Nilsson.
     p. 172
     ISBN 0-939666-76-6 (alk. paper): $14.95
     1. Botanists—Biography. 2. Plant collectors—Biography.
3. Botany—West (U.S.)—History—19th century. 4. Botany—
West (U.S.)—History—20th century. 5. Botany—West—
Nomenclature. I. Title.
QK26.N67 1994
581'.092'278—dc20   93-44015
                                                       CIP

Printed on recycled paper by Thomson-Shore, Inc., Dexter, Michigan

Table of Contents

FOREWORD

Like Adam naming the newly created plants and animals in the Garden of Eden, the botanists who first explored North America had the privilege of giving names to the plants they discovered as they wandered the wilds of the continent in a state of awe, wonder, and excitement. As late as a century ago, there were still vast areas of the American West where plants new to science were yet to be found and classified, and it was then that the botanical discovery movement reached a peak.

Many of these "unknown" plants had been named much earlier, of course, by the people who lived in the Americas before the European invasion, but to the world of botany they were still new and unclassified in the scientific lexicon. The earlier namings did not detract from the botanists' sense of discovery, and, in the same way, in the late twentieth century, our own personal experience with plants is not diminished and can only be enhanced by our knowledge of those botanists and their explorations. I can testify that my own sense of discovery was heightened immeasurably when I learned as I hiked over the poppy-sprinkled hills of the San Francisco Presidio that in precisely this place a botanist on a Russian expedition in 1815 had discovered and named the same California Poppy, now the official state flower.

The late Karen Nilsson was a discoverer in the sense that we can all be discoverers, adding to our personal identification of—and with—the plants and trees of our own region, wherever we might be. Her eager pursuit of knowledge of her natural environment and her intense sense of wonder illuminate her stories of the name-placing botanists and their adventures, from Lewis and Clark to Carl and Helen Sharsmith. Karen's perpetual curiosity about the natural world is infectious. Shining through these pages, it is her lasting legacy.

September 1993   *Harold Gilliam*

Collectors in the field.

PREFACE

While learning to identify wildflowers in the California Coast Ranges and the Sierra Nevada, I became curious. Was *Lewisia* first found on the Lewis and Clark expedition? Why is the pretty poppy saddled with a name like *Eschscholzia*? And who was Coulter of the pine with heavy cones?

Little did I realize when I set out to answer such questions that the annals of plant discovery are intimately linked to romantic tales of sailing expeditions, of solitary treks across barren deserts, and of eccentric collectors who would endure almost any hardship to uncover a new plant. Digging deeper, I discovered that these early collectors were part of a nineteenth-century botanical movement— a loosely linked network of European academics, East Coast professorial types, and a curious assortment of amateur botanists who preferred the wide open spaces of the undeveloped West to the "elegancies" of the more cultured East.

The men and women who made up this movement shared many characteristics. They were all risk-takers who valued the thrill of discovery over material wealth. The majority were either completely self-taught or had received just a smattering of plant study from inspired teachers. Several became interested in botany while studying the healing properties of plants in the short medical curriculum of the day. In the course of becoming doctors or "surgeon naturalists," their passion for plants overwhelmed their interest in disease.

Most of the scientifically trained botanists who headed this movement were men. Women's schools in the last century provided little science instruction to their students, particularly in such delicate subjects as plant reproduction. As a result, women expressed their interest in plants through painting, flower arranging, and nature study.

Another characteristic these nineteenth-century plant enthusiasts shared was longevity. More than a few lived well into their eighties, proof of John Muir's observation that "Longest is the life that contains the largest amount of time-effacing enjoyment—of work that is a steady delight."

This is a book of personal selection. Some of the people I have written about are world-renowned botanists. Others are scarcely remembered collectors. A personal interest in protecting biodiversity led me to include several figures whose lives are linked to the discovery and preservation of plants now on the brink of extinction. Each biographical sketch is accompanied by a drawing of a plant named in honor of that person. I have made a special effort to include illustrations of endangered species, knowing that you and your children may never have an opportunity to see these plants in the wild.

Karen B. Nilsson

INTRODUCTION

As you bend down to appreciate the beauty of a Lemmon's Paintbrush or to smile at the "mouse-tail" bracts emanating from a Douglas Fir cone, you are on the threshold of fascinating history. If only these tiny bits of nature could tell their own stories.

Those stories might begin in the distant past, when migrating ice-age hunters stumbled upon a "new world" and made it their own. Native Americans felt a deep reverence for plants, which they revered as spiritual, medicinal, and life-nourishing gifts from the Great Spirit.

The main thread of our botanical story, however, begins much later with the European discovery of the Americas. For European plant lovers, the age of discovery was a horticultural bonanza. The expeditions sent out to explore distant worlds returned to Europe with seeds, dried specimens, and living plants that soon enhanced royal botanical gardens and the estates of the landed gentry. European botanists reveled in the challenge of classifying and naming each new discovery.

In the early 1800s, a group of upstart Americans joined this scientific enterprise. After the American Revolution, Philadelphia was the center of botanical study in the infant republic. From there, leadership migrated to Princeton, Columbia, and Harvard universities and, eventually, westward to St. Louis. In each of these academic centers, "closet botanists" collected and catalogued specimens sent to them by plant explorers, army officers, self-taught naturalists, and pioneer settlers.

The great age of western plant collecting began in 1804, after the Louisiana Purchase doubled the size of the United States. That year, President Thomas Jefferson sent Lewis and Clark up the Missouri River in search of the elusive Northwest Passage. Before long, fur traders and mountain men, such as Jedediah Smith and Peter Ogden, were following other watersheds into the Rocky Mountains and beyond. They returned East with beaver pelts and tales of grand canyons, spurting geysers, deep granite valleys, and gigantic trees.

Economic depression in the 1840s spurred a population push westward. Year after year, covered wagons filled with hopeful emigrants rolled west along the Santa Fe, Oregon, and California trails to fresh starts. The 1849 California Gold Rush turned those rutted trails into dusty roads.

The federal government did its part to open the West to settlement by sponsoring expeditions to map western rivers, delineate boundaries, and scout transcontinental railroad routes. Many of these survey parties were led by military officers, often from the elite Corps of Topographical Engineers. One way or another, natural scientists, artists, and photographers with an interest in plant collecting found a place on these expeditions.

While Americans were pushing westward, one of those fascinating conjunctions of personalities and passions that often accelerates scientific progress triggered a botanical boom in the East. This flurry of scientific activity was shaped by the friendship and selflessness of three medical doctors—John Torrey, Asa Gray, and George Engelmann—who shared a love of plants.

Professor John Torrey taught at Columbia, West Point, and then Princeton, where he took the young Asa Gray under his wing and taught him the plant classification systems of the day. Torrey's energetic and visionary pupil dedicated his life to classification of plants, writing voluminous tracts and communicating with more than six hundred botanists and field collectors from his mecca at Harvard College.

Dr. George Engelmann lived and worked in that gateway to the West, St. Louis, Missouri. Engelmann acted as the frontier front man for his eastern colleagues, coordinating the collecting efforts of promising adventurers as they set out to explore the uncharted West. Engelmann's legacy lives on today in the pioneering work of the Missouri Botanical Garden in St. Louis.

For decades after their first meeting in 1840, these three men shared specimens, ideas, and a lifelong friendship. They were the interconnecting force that guided plant exploration and then captured the results in an enduring written record. To them fell the time-consuming task of comparing, identifying, describing, classifying, and, finally, naming each new discovery in both English and Latin. It was an enterprise that demanded amazing powers of mental discrimination and attention to detail. Once a collection had been studied, it had to be written up as well. Records show that these prolific scientists thought nothing of describing a collection of five hundred or more plants for a book or report on one expedition or another.

All three of these scientists depended on a network of amateur botanists to supply them with specimens of western plants. Most of these plant collectors collected for the sheer joy of discovery. Their only reward was the chance to have their names attached to a magnificent tree or a diminutive flower. A few turned collecting into a business, selling for a pittance the specimens they gathered.

By 1872, when the Escalante remained the only major river yet to be mapped in the United States, the botanical boom had peaked. Most of the West, by this time, had been thoroughly scoured by eager collectors. The pace of discovery slowed.

In the last years of the nineteenth century, prideful Westerners began to assert their expertise against that of the eastern scientific establishment. Botanists attached to the California Academy of Sciences in San Francisco maintained that they had the necessary knowledge of both the fine points of botany and their home landscape to name the plants they found. These pronouncements, of course, provoked an angry response from eastern academics.

By this time, however, botany itself was changing. With the development of better microscopes and the influence of Darwin's studies on evolution, botanical science was shifting away from classification toward research on plant physiology and ecology. Today, that focus is shifting again toward genetic studies and the preservation of biodiversity, particularly in fragile environments, such as tropical rain forests. Ethnobiology has become another active specialty as scientists work with indigenous peoples to record time-honored uses of wild plants before this knowledge is lost forever.

Despite these shifts, one thing remains constant in botany, and that is the excitement of collecting. In pursuit of something rare, plant collectors continue to climb a little higher or trek a little farther into wild places. The modern plant explorer's journey is often long and the rewards elusive. Still, the thrill of discovering a unique specimen or unusual flower is as great now as it was a century ago. The excitement is not yet over.

Vernon and Florence Bailey, Arizona 1920

THE COLLECTOR'S LOT

For the early plant collectors of the West, finding and preserving new plant species was an exhilarating and often exhausting enterprise. Travel across the western wilderness was never easy. One collector wrote of a day on the trail:

The company traveled thirty-three miles yesterday, drenched and bleached with rain and sleet, and chilled with a piercing wind; and then to finish the day we experienced the cooling, comfortless consolation of lying down wet without supper or fire. On such occasions I am liable to become fretful.

The best days were those spent collecting. Here, a member of a surveying party describes the work of the "plant men:"

After beans and scalding coffee, the fellows measuring the height of the peaks take off with their instruments, and we plant men climb along the water courses and tramp along the clefts looking for plants that we, and hopefully the esteemed Dr. Gray, have not seen before. The only textbook accompanying us is our memories of what we have learned from previous experience. When we spy a bright red mimulus that we hope is different from all others, we kneel by it, as if in prayer, and dig it up carefully down to its very bottom root. We carefully shake off the dirt and when possible wash it clean. Then we put it in our container called a vasculum and sling it over our shoulder. When we get back to camp our heavy burdens must be given our first attention.

Once found, samples of a new species had to be carefully pressed and dried for shipment east. Dr. George Engelmann of St. Louis wrote the following instructions to collectors on how best to preserve their discoveries:

Collect if possible several specimens of the same plant, partly to show different shades of the same species, and partly to be able to distribute them among diff. botanists. . . . It will be well to put your specimens in paper as soon as gathered; their parts are then fresh and still and are easily spread out in a neat way. . . . After the specimen has been put in paper and pressed a while, it becomes necessary to change the layers of paper as soon as they have become damp from the moisture absorbed from the plant and to substitute dry ones for them. This ought to be repeated daily till the specimen is completely dried. . . . When you have got a sufficiently sized bundle together, pack it either in a box of convenient size or in a fresh skin of some animal (hair inside) which will harden and shrink and form an easily handled and safe package.

The drying process sounds easy enough. But, in fact, preserving plants was a tedious chore. Witness the problems of this collector:

We sit for hours before a hot camp fire, with the sweat pouring down our face, to completely dry our papers and plants. How I wish the plants dried at once, but often it takes several days and sometimes a week. The faster they dry, the better they retain their color. Each day we must press them between dry paper. And what misery when it rains; then nothing or no one is dry! When it is windy our scarce paper blows out into the meadows.

Still, the plant collector's lot was not all hardship and frustration. Exploring for plants could also be a wondrous adventure. Wrote one happy collector of the rewards of his work:

Every step I take into the fields, groves, and hills appears to afford new enjoyments. Here is an old acquaintance seen again; there a novelty. I hasten to pluck it, admire it, and put it in my pack. I feel an exultation. I am going to add a new object, or a page to science. This peaceful conquest has cost no tears, but fills my mind with a proud sensation of not being useless on earth, of having detected another link of the creative power of God.

A bit about naming plants

Anyone can name a plant not previously classified by following the legalistic steps outlined in the International Code of Botanical Nomenclature. An outline of the new plant's botanical description must be published in Latin in a reputable journal, and a type specimen, or sample of the plant, must reside in an herbarium for others to study.

The convention of using two Latin words to describe plants originated with the Swedish botanist Carl Linnaeus in the 1730s. The first word identifies the group, or genus, to which the plant belongs. The second identifies the particular species. Either word may commemorate the collector who discovered the plant, where the plant was found, or some special feature of the plant. The choice rests with the namer.

Botanical Latin has its own rules. When a species is named for a man whose name ends in a vowel, add the letter *i*. If the man's name ends in a consonant, the usual practice is to add *ii*. If the plant is being named for a woman, add *ae*. Even when all the rules are followed, the naming of plants still generates controversy between botanists known as "lumpers," who prefer plant groupings that encompass a variety of characteristics, and "splitters," who separate plants into new species based on only slight differences. The illustrious Asa Gray wrote about the difficulties in making such discriminations. From his words, we can begin to appreciate the skill and knowledge of the professional botanist.

> *People generally suppose that species, and even genera, are like coin from the mint, or bank notes from the printing press, each with its fixed marks and signature. . . . But in fact species are judgments—judgments of variable value, and often very fallible judgments, as we botanists well know. And genera are more obviously judgments, and more and more liable to be affected by new discoveries. Judgments formed today—perhaps with full confidence, perhaps with misgiving—may tomorrow with the discovery of new materials or the detecting of some before unobserved point of structure, have to be weighed and decided anew.*

Meriwether Lewis

Wm. Clark

Meriwether Lewis
1774–1809

William Clark
1770–1838

In the early nineteenth century, Lewis and Clark's expedition across the uncharted West captured the American imagination, much as space voyages do today. Inspired by visions of a water route to the Pacific and dreams of opening the newly acquired Louisiana Purchase for settlement, President Thomas Jefferson asked his protégé and private secretary, Meriwether Lewis, to lead an expedition across the western half of the continent.

To complement his administrative skills, Lewis chose William Clark, a friend and experienced woodsman, to help lead the trip. The two recruited a scraggly band of soldiers and rivermen, Clark's slave, York, and a Newfoundland dog to make the journey. Along the way, they were joined by a French-Canadian trapper, his sixteen-year-old Shoshone wife, Sacajawea, and their newborn son.

No one in the group was a scientist by profession, although Lewis was given a crash course in natural history in Philadelphia before the expedition left St. Louis in the spring of 1804. The explorers took with them detailed instructions from Jefferson to observe and record "the soil and face of the country," to note its "growth & vegetable productions," and to collect any animals thought to be "rare or extinct." Lewis and Clark followed these instructions faithfully, recording what they saw with remarkable accuracy, though in a not very elegant style.

The explorers' epic journey to the Pacific Ocean and back took almost two and a half years. In that time, they traveled nearly eight thousand miles by boat, horse, and foot, a distance equivalent to a quarter of the way around the globe. Unfortunately, there was no national museum to house the treasure trove of specimens and artifacts Lewis and Clark brought back to St. Louis. As a result, the collection was dispersed. Some of the plants went to England, where they were described with little credit going to their discoverers.

This may explain why so few of the plants first collected by Lewis and Clark bear their names. One that does is *Lewisia rediviva,* or Bitterroot, now the state flower of Montana. Lewis observed the Shoshone digging up the plants and reported that the root "had a very bitter taste, which was naucious to my pallate." One wonders if this is the plant he would have chosen to be named for himself.

Clark, however, would probably be pleased by the naming of *Clarkia amoena* in his honor. He described this member of the Evening Primrose Family as "a beautiful herbaceous plant." The raucous high-mountain bird first called Clark's Crow and now Clark's Nutcracker bears his name as well. The Judith Mountains of Montana were named for Clark's sweetheart back home, and to balance things out, the Marias River was named for the girl Lewis left behind.

The explorers' journals and drawings were left untouched until Clark shepherded them into print in 1814 with financial support from the wealthy banker Nicholas Biddle. The published journals gave Americans their first look at the vast territory added to the United States by the Louisiana Purchase. The Rocky Mountains were described for the first time, along with the curious Continental Divide, where, at certain high points, some waters flowed east to the Atlantic Ocean and others west to the Pacific.

With the publication of Lewis and Clark's journals, Americans finally were able to look westward with some sense of reality as to the distance and hazards involved in transcontinental travel. The impact must have been sobering. Thirty years would pass before another botanical collector finally ventured overland to the Pacific.

Bitterroot, *Lewisia rediviva*

A low-growing perennial plant in the Purslane Family, found in rocky areas from British Columbia to southern California and east into Montana, Colorado, and Arizona. The rosy (deep pink to whitish) flowers have many petals and often bloom before the narrow, succulent leaves appear. The roots are large and fleshy. This genus is native to western North America and has eighteen species.

Farewell to Spring, *Clarkia amoena*

A lavender to purplish red flower, often with a darker center. Each of the four fan-shaped petals grows up to an inch long. Usually a slender plant, but may be branched. Grows in grassy fields and slopes at low elevations, from Washington to Baja California and into Arizona.

Lewisia
rediviva

Clarkia amoena

A.H.

3

Adelbert d. Chamisso

Adelbert von Chamisso
1781-1838

Johann Friedrich Gustav von Eschscholtz
1793-1831

California has quite rightly been called the Golden State, with its dried grasses covering autumn hills, masses of yellow tidy tip flowers carpeting spring meadows, and veins of precious metal running through the Mother Lode. When gold seekers flocked to California in 1849, they did not take long to find their own golden mementos of this new land. They pressed the California Poppy and sent the dried flowers in their letters home.

By the turn of this century, flower lovers were lobbying for the orange poppy, which is limited to the Pacific Coast, to become California's state flower. The legislature gave this official status to *Eschscholzia* in 1903. Perfect as the poppy may be as a state symbol, it will never win a popularity contest based on its botanical name. One outspoken botanist has complained that a college course is needed just to pronounce *Eschscholzia*.

The story of this tongue-twisting name takes us back to California's days of discovery. In the fall of 1817, the Russian ship *Rurik* followed the wind into San Francisco Bay. Officially, the ship was there to reprovision while searching for the elusive Northwest Passage. Very likely, the *Rurik*'s captain also wanted to assess the strength of the Spanish military garrison at the San Francisco Presidio.

On board the Russian ship was a self-taught botanist, writer, and poet named Adelbert von Chamisso. Chamisso was born in France, but the dislocations of the French Revolution had driven his family to Prussia when he was just a boy. There, the sensitive young poet grew up feeling like a man without a country. This sense of rootlessness may have inspired Chamisso to write his best-loved work, a tale about a man who loses his shadow, titled *Peter Schlemihl's Remarkable Story*.

In 1815, Chamisso boarded the *Rurik* to join a Russian exploring expedition in the role of naturalist. His collecting apparel was described by a colleague as

> *antique garb, once the state dress of a South Sea Chief, much worn, mended, and stained, with a black cap of cloth or velvet, a large green box suspended by leather straps over his back, and a short pipe in his mouth, together with a rude tobacco pouch.*

Johann Friedrich Gustav von Eschscholtz

Here, indeed, was the European romantic stepping ashore to explore the new world.

Stepping ashore with the poet-botanist was the ship's surgeon, Johann Friedrich Gustav von Eschscholtz, a young doctor from the Baltic port of Dorpat. Chamisso described his friend as "almost reserved, but true and noble as gold."

Today, few wildflower enthusiasts would expect to find much of anything blooming in San Francisco at the end of California's six-month rainless period. But poppies pop up at unexpected times, and near the Presidio, the two visitors' eyes were caught by a bright orange flower. Chamisso put his friend's name into history books that fall day by attaching *Eschscholz* to the poppy and to more than thirty other new species collected around San Francisco Bay.

A decade later, Dr. Eschscholtz, then a professor of zoology at Dorpat, returned to California on another sea voyage. He used this occasion to repay Chamisso for past honors by naming a showy blue bush found blooming near the coast *Lupinus Chamissonis*.

Today, blue and gold are the official colors of California. How fitting that the golden poppy and blue lupine still evoke memories of two of the state's earliest naturalist-visitors.

California Poppy, *Eschscholzia californica*

Easily distinguished by four brilliant orange, satiny petals. Annual or perennial plant, with finely divided, gray-green leaves, bearing many flowers on branching stems. Blooms from March through May on hillsides and in valleys across California, with similar species found in Arizona, Utah, and Nevada.

Blue Beach Lupine, *Lupinus Chamissonis*

Erect shrub with many short, leafy branches belonging to the Pea Family. Blue flowers marked with a yellow spot on the upper petal appear in two- to six-inch clusters from March to June. Grows on sandy beaches and dunes along the California coast, from north of San Francisco to Los Angeles.

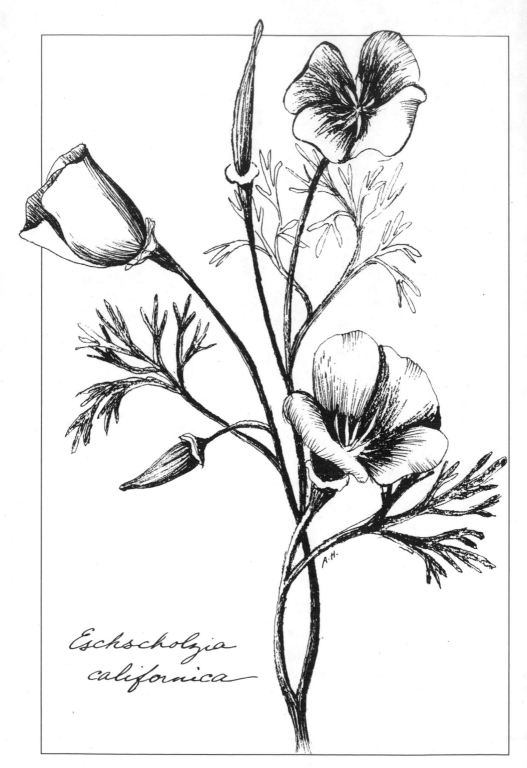

Eschscholzia
californica

Lupinus Chamissonis

Wm.P Hooker

Sir J.D. and Mrs. Hooker

William Hooker
1785-1865

Joseph Hooker
1817-1911

Peter Raven
1936-

A solitary shrub, the only one of its kind growing in San Francisco's Presidio, bears the name *Arctostaphylos Hookeri ssp. Ravenii*. William and Joseph Hooker and Peter Raven, though separated by a century and the Atlantic Ocean, all contributed to the building of world-class botanical institutions. From the efforts of the Hookers, father and son, came the rebirth of the Royal Botanical Gardens at Kew near London; and through his work, Peter Raven has earned the leadership role of the Missouri Botanical Gardens in St. Louis in international plant-conservation efforts. By an odd coincidence, their names appear together on this one Manzanita bush.

Sir William Hooker spent the early part of his career as a professor of botany at the University of Glasgow, where he was known as an expert in mosses, ferns, and fungi. From there, he organized many of the collectors who were sent out to explore the Pacific Northwest, at that time controlled by Hudson's Bay Company. Hooker gave direction to the Scottish explorer David Douglas and received an early collection of plants from the English printer-turned-collector Thomas Nuttall. Asa Gray, America's leading botanist, spent several weeks studying with Hooker in Glasgow. Hooker honored that association by naming the genus *Grayia* for his American colleague.

In response to a critical report from Parliament about the disintegration of the Royal Botanical Gardens, William Hooker agreed to become the first director of Kew Gardens in 1841. Under Sir William's leadership, which lasted until his death in 1865, Kew Gardens became a leading research facility with study gardens, an herbarium, a library, and a museum.

Joseph Hooker succeeded his father as director of Kew Gardens and remained in that position for two decades. Earlier in his career, the younger Hooker had traveled the world around, gathering material for works on the flora of Antarctica, the Himalayas, India, New Zealand, and North Africa. From these studies, Sir Joseph developed an enduring interest in plant geography and in the relationship of American and Asian plants. As a friend of Charles

Darwin, he helped apply evolutionary theory to plant distribution and variation.

In 1877, Joseph Hooker, then president of the Royal Society of London, made a historic visit to the United States as a guest of Asa Gray. The two friends traveled across the country by rail as botanical tourists, meeting with American plant enthusiasts along the way. Though both in their sixties, they climbed Gray's and Torrey's peaks in Colorado. In California, they joined flower-seeking excursions led by John Muir, whom they teased for being "so eternally enthusiastic." Around the campfire, Hooker regaled his American friends with stories of his adventures in the Himalayas, while admitting that "no forest on the globe rivaled the great coniferous forest of [Muir's] much-loved Sierra." Sir Joseph returned home to Kew Gardens with a thousand new specimens for his study of plant distribution.

Nearly a century later, a San Francisco teenager named Peter Raven began his botanical career by riding the streetcar to out-of-the-way places to collect plants. On one of his excursions, he found an unusual Manzanita bush on the Presidio Army Base and took a sample to Alice Eastwood at the California Academy of Sciences. Eastwood helped Raven determine that he had found a new sub-species of *Arctostaphylos Hookeri,* which she proceeded to name for its discoverer. Like Joseph Hooker, Peter Raven went on to study the flora of New Zealand, where he is still remembered for his perseverance in getting up at dawn to study the pollinating habits of the Evening Primrose.

Raven's career, like Sir Joseph's, has encompassed both adventure and administration. Today, Raven serves as director of the Missouri Botanical Gardens, where he is highly regarded for putting this institution at the forefront of efforts to preserve tropical rain forests and conserve endangered species.

Hooker's Evening Primrose, *Oenothera Hookeri*

A tall, red-stemmed, sturdy plant producing an abundance of bright yellow, largish flowers from July through October. Grows from coastal beaches up into the mixed-evergreen forests of the California Coast Ranges, from Humboldt south to San Luis Obispo County and in Arizona at elevations of 3,500 to 9,500 feet.

Oenothera Hookeri

A·H·

1846

DAVID DOUGLAS

AN EMINENT BOTANIST WHO CLASSIFIED
OREGON FOREST TREES, WAS BORN IN
SCOTLAND IN 1799. BEING A LOVER OF
NATURE, HE SPENT SEVEN YEARS IN
BOTANICAL GARDENS AND BECAME A
TRUSTED COLLECTOR. HENCE HE WAS
SENT TO OREGON, ARRIVING AT FORT
VANCOUVER, APRIL 17, 1825. HE STUD-
IED THE FLORA OF THIS COUNTRY TWO
YEARS AND STARTED TO ENGLAND, MAR.
27, 1827. HE RETURNED TO OREGON IN
1829-1833, AND WAS KILLED BY A WILD
BULLOCK NEAR HILO, HAWAII, IN 1834.

OREGON PIONEER
ASSOCIATION

46th Annual Reunion
Thursday, June 20
1918

Ribbon celebrating David Douglas

David Douglas
1799–1834

Around the turn of the nineteenth century, British horticultural explorers were sending sun-loving exotic plants from equatorial countries to their cool-weather homeland in the hope that they would survive in glass conservatories. In 1823, David Douglas was the first collector to be sent to gather new plants in a temperate area with moisture patterns similar to those in the British Isles. The many tree and flower seeds he sent home were soon flourishing in their adopted land.

A rowdy, independent, and "singularly abstemious" boy, who walked twelve miles round-trip to school each day, Douglas ended his formal education when he was ten. He was apprenticed to the head gardener at a Scottish estate and, by the age of eighteen, had become an expert horticulturist. Douglas spent another three years studying at the Glasgow Botanical Gardens, where he worked with Professor William Hooker (later to become the director of the Royal Botanical Gardens at Kew). Hooker recommended Douglas to the Horticultural Society of London as an able collector who was eager to travel. The society first planned to send Douglas to China, but unsettled political conditions there forced him to cancel his trip. To keep their collector employed, the society shipped him off to the United States to collect plants that would grow outdoors in England.

Between 1823 and his death eleven years later, Douglas's life was consumed by three collecting expeditions to North America. The first took him to the East Coast and included a visit to Niagara Falls. A year later, he embarked on an eight-month voyage around the tip of South America. After weathering weeks of fearsome storms, his ship finally landed at the mouth of the Columbia, the mighty river that separates present-day Oregon and Washington states. At that time, the only Europeans in this region were a handful of fur trappers manning trading posts for the Hudson's Bay Company.

The Columbia became Douglas's highway into this verdant region. He spent months at a time in the forest, collecting alone or with native guides who called him "the grass man." Foul weather was a constant problem. Douglas later wrote that

> *I laboured under very great disadvantage by the almost continual rain; many of my specimens I lost, and although I had several oilcloths, I was unable to keep my plants and my blanket dry.*

At the end of a day of collecting, it was not uncommon for Douglas to find himself wet to the skin, suffering from an infected knee, and worrying about his deteriorating eyesight. At times like these, he did what any good Scotsman would do. He heated water over a fire and brewed his national drink, "tea, which is the monarch of all foods after fatiguing journeys."

Douglas made one sortie after another up the Columbia into the Blue Mountains, the Walla Walla area, and the Spokane River Valley. His travels took him north into Idaho and ended with a walk across Canada. Traveling by foot, Indian canoe, and on horseback, the tireless collector covered more than six thousand miles in two years.

On his third trip to America, in 1830, Douglas struck out in new directions. For a year and a half, he trekked across California, where he visited Mexican missions and discovered the Douglas Fir. He described this tree in his journal as "one of the most striking and truly graceful objects in nature."

From California, Douglas traveled north and was nearly drowned in a canoe accident on the Fraser River in British Columbia. His next stop was Hawaii. There, Douglas met his maker in a freak accident on the slopes of Mauna Loa. While climbing the volcano, he fell into a pit and was fatally gored by a wild bull.

In his short lifetime, Douglas proved to be a resilient and tenacious collector who gained lasting respect on both sides of the Atlantic. Wherever he ventured in the forested Northwest, Douglas spied conifers not known in his homeland nor in the eastern United States. He once wrote his mentor, Dr. Hooker, "You must think I manufacture pines at my pleasure." In addition to the Douglas Fir, he discovered the Sitka Spruce, seven pines—including the Sugar Pine—and another seven firs. Douglas also collected many flowers, such as penstemons, godetias, and the Douglas iris that were soon blooming in English gardens. It is said of David Douglas that no other collector has reaped such a harvest or has had his name associated with so many useful plants.

Douglas Fir, *Pseudotsuga Mentziesii*

A magnificent tall, straight forest conifer. Long pendulous branches, slender needles, and cones with conspicuous bracts between thinnish scales. The most important lumber tree of North America. Grows in mixed-evergreen forests, from British Columbia to northern California.

Douglas Fir

Thomas Drummond

Thomas Drummond
1790–1835

Thomas Drummond and David Douglas had much in common. Both were Scottish naturalists who came to the attention of Sir William Hooker at the University of Glasgow. Both were sent out by British horticultural institutions to collect plants in the New World. Both displayed remarkable tenacity, dedication to their tasks, and, some might say, Scottish self-reliance as they pursued their goals in the face of grueling hardships. And both met untimely ends on tropical islands as they began their journeys home. But while Douglas stalked the towering conifers in the mountainous Pacific Northwest, Drummond tramped the flat plains of Texas looking for less lofty species.

Thomas Drummond launched his collecting career in 1825, when he joined Sir John Franklin's second overland expedition to Canada. The explorers spent two years charting Canada's Arctic coast, making extensive journeys inland along the Coppermine and Mackenzie rivers. Drummond returned to Great Britain with his finds to become the curator of the Botanical Garden at Belfast and to write a comprehensive book on mosses.

In 1833, Sir William Hooker sent Drummond on what turned out to be a disastrous trip to Texas. From the start, this collecting expedition was upset by plagues of man and nature. An epidemic of cholera struck the Gulf Coast settlements that year, and in a short time, everyone traveling with Drummond was dead from the pestilence. Drummond deemed himself lucky to have escaped a similar fate, writing that

> *Though ignorant of the nature of the disease and the proper remedies, I fortunately took what was proper for me, and in a few hours the violent cramps in my legs gave way to the opium with which I dosed myself.*

The weather, too, seemed out of control. Early summer storms swamped the Gulf Plain, leading to widespread flooding known as the "Great Overflow." Drummond wrote home to Hooker that the Rio Brazos "had risen to a height so unprecedented, that a boat brought me across the prairies, which were flooded to a depth of from nine to fifteen feet!" The wet weather destroyed a third of the plants Drummond had collected, and he gave fair warning to his patron that "it is impossible for me to collect anything like a given number of species in a certain time."

Drummond was understandably critical of Texas, and his comments to this effect irritated pioneers attempting to settle the Gulf Coast. Yet, he must have seen redeeming features in the land

and its people, for he wrote that he hoped to bring his family back to Texas to live. Fate would not have it so. On his journey home, Drummond died of fever in Cuba.

Before his untimely death, Drummond sent 150 specimens of birds and more than 700 plants and seeds, including a beautiful phlox, back to Hooker in Glasgow. Hooker named the lovely flower *Phlox Drummondii* "that it may serve as a frequent memento of its unfortunate discoverer." As you enjoy our garden varieties of phlox, you might pause to remember that their introduction to cultivation was thanks to the persistent Thomas Drummond.

Drummond's Phlox, *Phlox Drummondii*

An annual wildflower of Texas and nearby states that has clusters of reddish purple flowers topping slender stems. A member of the Phlox Family.

Phlox
Drummondii

A.H.

21

Thomas Coulter

Thomas Coulter
1793–1843

Ever since St. Patrick ran the snakes out of Ireland, at least some Irish have had a way with these reptiles. As a young botany student, Thomas Coulter became fascinated with snakes and lizards. One of his teachers, the renowned French botanist Augustine Pyrame de Candolle, reminisced that Coulter kept reptiles in his pockets and whistled tunes to them to keep them still.

The Scottish naturalist David Douglas found other reasons to be impressed with Coulter, noting that he was a superior salmon fisherman, "besides being a beautiful shot with a rifle, nearly as successful as myself." This was high praise, indeed, as Douglas was known for his ability to shoot down cones from the tops of Sugar Pines.

Thomas Coulter's outdoor skills were of inestimable value in the life of adventure he chose for himself. After training to become a doctor in Ireland and then studying botany in Geneva under Professor de Candolle, he accepted a post as doctor in a Mexican mining camp. Arriving in 1825, Coulter was one of the earliest scientists to collect in this country, which had recently freed itself from Spanish domination. He spent ten years managing mines and pursuing get-rich schemes, none of which panned out.

Deciding to concentrate for a time on plant collecting, Coulter sailed north to California, where he met the intrepid Douglas. The latter described Coulter as "a man eminently calculated to work, full of zeal, very amiable and I hope may do much good to Science." The two naturalists collected together in the fall of 1831 and the spring of 1832. It was then that Coulter described the "peculiar ponderous coned pine which now bears the name Coulter's Pine." Perhaps he followed Douglas's lead and shot the heavy, seed-laden cones down from the tall pines with his rifle.

Being used to the arid mountains and deserts of Mexico, Coulter took a fast walk across a hundred miles of California desert to become the first botanist to collect in Arizona. Along the way, he found the Matilija Poppy growing near the San Luis River. The British botanist who later named this plant *Romneya Coulteri,* wrote that he would have named the genus *Coulteri,* but such a genus already existed. That being the case, he reported:

> I desire, as the next greatest respect that I can pay to Dr. Coulter's memory, to bestow upon this fine plant of his discovery, the name of his most distinguished and one of his most intimate friends. I inscribe it to Rev. T. Romney Robinson, the Astronomer of Armagh.

Coulter returned to Mexico after two years in California, only to be beset by revolution, cholera, and dishonest business partners. In 1834, he went home to Dublin, where Trinity College accepted his gift of fifty thousand herbarium specimens and made him curator of the collection. Coulter spent his remaining days in the green, rain-drenched land of his birth, poring over the plants he had collected in the arid North American West.

Matilija Poppy, *Romneya Coulteri*

A beautiful, stout perennial with large white, crinkly petaled flowers showing many bright yellow stamens. Native to southern California. Found inland from the coast in dry washes and canyons below 4,000 feet, often with chaparral.

Romneya Coulteri

John Torrey

John Torrey
1796–1873

"That represents a deal of back-ache," reflected John Torrey about his herbarium and, no doubt, about his long life as one of America's leading botanists. Even into his last years, Torrey continued to burn the midnight oil, poring over his plant collections at Columbia College. And yet, for Torrey, botany was "only" an avocation tucked into his long career as a professor of chemistry.

By the early 1800s, American science was moving away from generalist natural philosophers, such as Benjamin Franklin, toward specialization. Torrey earned a medical degree in 1818 and became a professor six years later. For several years, he was simultaneously teaching at Columbia, West Point, and Princeton, shuttling his family among the three schools. After one of these moves, Torrey wrote of his ailing wife, Eliza, that "She is always in poor health for a few days after a change of residence." Besides teaching, he served as the supervisor of the New York Mint, using his skills to help get the wealth of California's Gold Rush into the money stream.

Even with all his other responsibilities, Torrey still found time for his plants. The United States government was just beginning to look west of the Mississippi River when Torrey entered the field of botany. Only pockets of the West had been explored. California and Texas were still provinces of Mexico, and Oregon was controlled by British fur traders. While Torrey was fascinated by these distant lands, he never headed west with the explorers. He once admitted that "I have not herberized out of a circle of 400 miles radius" of New York City, adding that "This is a rather sad confession for a North American botanist."

Torrey's contribution to botany was not as a collector but as a plant taxonomist. He was the first American to adopt the "natural system" of classification, using it to describe the plants sent to him by Edwin James in the 1820s. In Europe, the natural scheme, based on the structure and function of plants, had already begun to replace the Linnean system, which classifies plants on the basis of male and female parts. Torrey commented later that "The Linnean system will go down and I should not like to be the last to prop it up."

Torrey's botanical reputation grew rapidly as Americans began to penetrate the uncharted West. Each new expedition yielded boxes of specimens, most of which were sent back East for Torrey to study and classify. Torrey's name appears on the reports of the Wilkes Expedition, Lieutenant John Frémont's explorations, the Mexican Boundary Expedition, and Pacific railroad survey expeditions.

In the mid-1830s, young Asa Gray came to New York to study with Torrey, who by then stood at the center of American botany. Eliza Torrey, known for her intellect and knowledge of languages and culture, became Gray's teacher in the civilized arts. Dr. Torrey became his scientific mentor, making Gray his chemistry lab assistant. The two men became close friends and lifelong botanical colleagues. While they were both on their way up professionally, they coauthored *Flora of North America,* a landmark botanical work that never was finished completely in their lifetimes.

Anyone who has been to San Diego knows the windswept Torrey Pine, which hangs on to the cliffs north of the city. In 1850, Joseph L. LeConte pointed out the unusual conifer to plant explorer Charles C. Parry. The latter wrote to Torrey:

> *I here found a new species of pine growing in sheltered places about the bluff. Its characters are so unique I am in hopes it may be non-descript . . . if new I wish it with your permission to bear the name of Pinus Torreyana.*

In appreciation of the key role John Torrey played in furthering American botanical studies, Parry also named a peak in the Rocky Mountains for him. A year before Torrey died, he and one of his daughters visited Parry in the Rockies, traveling by carriage to his camp at nearly twelve thousand feet. Parry wrote of that visit:

> *It was my privilege to entertain this distinguished guest at my rude botanical retreat in the heart of the Rocky Mountains. Here, in close proximity to my cabin, I could point out to him many of the living plants that he had described fifty years previously, from herbarium specimens, but had never before seen in their living beauty.*

High winds and "rare air" prevented Torrey from ascending to the top of the peak named in his honor. Still, he was able "to gaze on its sky-piercing summit and to snatch from its wintry slopes some late-grown floral mementos of his early labors."

Torrey Pine, *Pinus Torreyana*

A small pine with branching trunk and long needles, five to a bundle. Cones are 4 to 6 inches long and quite broad, with each scale thickening to a knob. This rare pine grows in two colonies, one on Santa Rosa Island, the other near Del Mar in San Diego County, California.

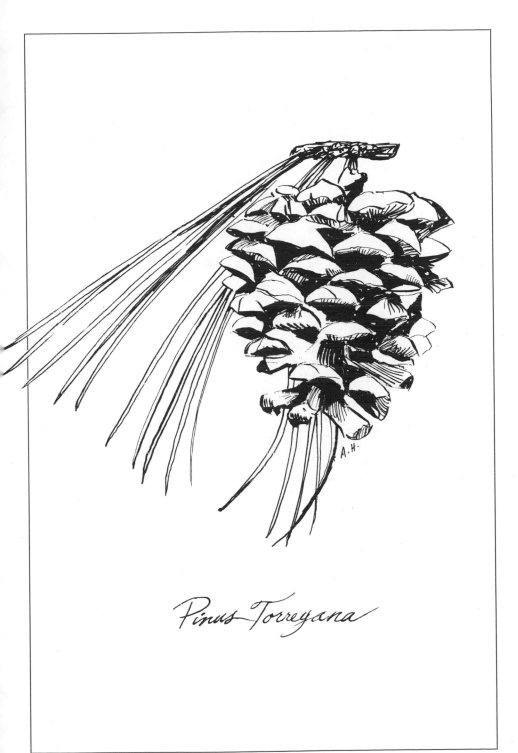

Pinus Torreyana

Edwin James

Today's national heroes are often sports figures whose fame may be measured in millions of dollars. After a short burst of glory, most fade from view and are soon forgotten. A daring peak-climber of 150 years ago named Edwin James made only civil-servant wages. Yet, his memory lingers on in the genus *Jamesia*.

By the age of twenty-three, James had studied medicine, graduated from Middlebury College, and gone to New York to learn botany from Professor John Torrey. His knowledge of both medicine and plants led to his appointment in 1820 as the naturalist-surgeon for the federal government's Yellowstone Expedition. Led by Stephen Long, this expedition explored the Rocky Mountains, from the Yellowstone country south into New Mexico.

While exploring the Colorado Rockies, James and two colleagues became the first Americans to ascend the towering fourteen thousand-foot peak that was later named for the explorer Zebulon Pike. Pike's Peak was a tough climb. The first night on the slopes, the climbing party could not find a flat place to camp. James wrote that they "were under the necessity of securing ourselves from rolling into the brook by means of a pole placed against two trees." In this manner, "We passed an uneasy night."

The view from the top, however, must have been thrilling. "As the sun rose majestically above the well-defined horizon of the plains," wrote James, "the resemblance to a wide open sea was strikingly manifested." He observed that the summit "is covered to a great depth with large splintery fragments of a rock," which he attributed to the effects of lightning.

James was the first plant collector to explore the Rocky Mountains and to describe the treeless tundra found at high elevations. After sending his many specimens to Professor Torrey for study, he also became the first American collector to have his discoveries described using the new natural system of classification. Forty years later, botanist Charles C. Parry noted these contributions when he named a peak on the Continental Divide in James's honor.

Among the many plants discovered by James was a large species of Mountain Columbine. "It is heretofore unknown to the Flora of the United States to which it forms a splendid acquisition," he wrote. "If it should appear not to be described, it may receive the name of *Aquilegia coerulea*." This Rocky Mountain columbine, similar to the garden species, later became Colorado's state flower. James was struck by the striking coloration of these and other high-altitude flowers and wondered if the deep blue of the sky had an influence in producing a like color in the flowers.

After the adventures of his youth, James settled into a very different kind of life. He moved to a farm in Iowa, where he edited a temperance newspaper and became something of a mystic and a recluse. He was also an active abolitionist, serving as a conductor of runaway slaves on the Underground Railroad. Still, James never forgot the pleasures of collecting. A few years before he died, he wrote to Torrey that

> *It enters into my day dreams that I may yet go forth to gather weeds and stones and rubbish for the use of some who may value such things, and perhaps drop this life-wearied body beside some solitary stream in the wilderness.*

Waxflower, *Jamesia americana*

An erect, much-branched shrub similar to mock orange. This ancient plant, the only one of its genus, is also called Wild Hydrangea. Grows on rocky ledges high in the southern Sierra Nevada, the desert mountain ranges of California, and western Nevada.

Jamesia americana

Thomas Nuttall

From the moment he first viewed America's eastern seaboard in 1808, the young English printer Thomas Nuttall looked forward to the day he could wander "over the wild domain of primeval nature and behold Another Flora of bolder hues." Nuttall's curiosity about unfamiliar plants led him to Professor Benjamin S. Barton, a leading light of the Philadelphia Academy of Sciences. Barton gave the shy young man access to his library and then sent him westward with the parting words: "Next to your personal safety, science, and not mere conveniency in traveling, is the great object of the journey."

Nuttall joined a party of trappers sent west by John Jacob Astor in 1811 to build a trading base at the mouth of the Columbia River. The expedition traversed much of the same territory that Lewis and Clark had explored only a few years before. The rugged trappers shook their heads at the antics of the plant-happy naturalist, especially when he used the barrel of his gun to dig up roots. After reaching the Pacific Coast, Nuttall returned with his specimens and seeds to England, where he received little credit for these early discoveries, except for the lovely *Calochortus Nuttallii,* or Sego Lily.

Nuttall soon returned to the United States to resume his explorations. This time, he headed across the flowery Oklahoma plains in an attempt to reach the southern Rocky Mountains. Along the way, a severe fever stopped him nearly dead in his tracks. Had it not been for his guide, he might not have made it back to civilization. By now, Nuttall was gaining a reputation as a blessed fool, who wandered about with single-minded intensity, nearly always half-starved, sick, or lost.

In 1818, Nuttall made his name in botany by typesetting and self-publishing *Genera of North American Plants,* a book based on his own careful observations of the native flora. His reputation established, the printer-turned-botanist was attracted to Harvard College, where he lectured in natural history and served as curator of its botanical garden. After a decade of academic life, however, Nuttall resigned, saying that he preferred to work "not in the closet but in the field."

Nuttall's chance to resume field work came in 1834, when he embarked on another overland trek to Oregon, this one led by his friend Nathaniel Wyeth. Once on the Pacific Coast, Nuttall sailed twice to Hawaii, returning the second time to Monterey, California. He could not have arrived at a lovelier moment. "The early spring had spread out its varied carpet of flowers," he wrote. "All of them had to me the charm of novelty, and many were adorned with the most brilliant and varied hues."

From Monterey, Nuttall made his way south to San Diego, where he was recognized by a Harvard student who had left school for a taste of the sea-faring life. This young man, Richard Henry Dana, later described Nuttall in his journal, *Two Years Before the Mast,* as

> *sort of an oldish man with white hair, [who] spent all his time in the bush, along the beach, picking up flowers and shells, and such truck, and had a dozen boxes and barrels, full of them. . . . The* Pilgrim*'s crew christened Mr. N. "Old Curious," from his zeal for curiosities, and some of them said he was crazy, and that his friends let him go about and amuse himself in this way.*

After returning East, Nuttall was beset with financial worries. In 1841, he reluctantly accepted an English uncle's legacy of a small estate, conditioned on his residing there. Nuttall wrote that

> *I prefer the wilds of America a thousand times. . . . But the "oft-told tale" approaches to its close and I must now bid a long adieu to the "new world," its sylvan scenes, its mountains, wilds and plains; and henceforth, in the evening of my career, I return, almost an exile in the land of my nativity.*

While living in America, Nuttall was often miffed by the lack of support he got for his collecting expeditions. Nonetheless, as this tribute by the famed botanist Asa Gray attests, he was appreciated in his adopted country. In Gray's estimation,

> *No botanist has visited so large a portion of the United States, or made such an amount of observations in the field and forest. Probably few naturalists have ever excelled him in aptitude for such observations, in quickness of eye, tact in discrimination, and tenacity of memory.*

Sego Lily, *Calochortus Nuttallii*

An erect, slender stem, with a few narrow leaves from a bulb. One to four widely flaring, bowl-like flowers have three white petals marked with lilac or yellow and with hairs and a dark spot around the glands near the base. Fairly common on the western Great Plains, from southwestern North Dakota into northern Arizona and New Mexico. The state flower of Utah.

Calochortus Nuttallii

37

Nathaniel Wyeth

Nathaniel Wyeth
1802–1856

Nathaniel Wyeth was a nineteenth-century entrepreneur. He began his business career by cutting ice on New England ponds for shipment to China, Ceylon, and the Caribbean. He made the task more efficient by inventing a two-horse saw that cut deep, smooth blocks of standard size. But Wyeth's ambitions were not frozen by the ice industry. In 1832, he organized a fur-trading expedition to Oregon, a territory much praised for its timber and agricultural potential. He financed the expedition by putting together a joint-stock venture for participants who could join the trip for forty dollars in expenses. Wyeth sent his heavy freight to the mouth of the Columbia by ship, while he personally led an overland party to Oregon.

Nothing worked out as the young businessman had hoped. The trapper hired in St. Louis to guide the 1832 expedition quit along the way, leaving the inexperienced Wyeth to manage the rest of the journey on his own. Only a remnant of the original party completed the trek to the mouth of the Columbia River. There, Wyeth learned that the ship carrying his trading provisions had been lost in the Hawaiian Islands. Furthermore, the fur trade had by then peaked, and profits were hard to come by.

After wintering at a Hudson's Bay Company post, Wyeth and two companions headed back to Boston in the spring of 1833. When they reached the Flathead River in Idaho, Wyeth "went out to collect some flowers for friend Nuttall" back at Harvard College, perhaps hoping to forget his failures. In a letter written to accompany the specimens, Wyeth commented to Thomas Nuttall:

> I have sent through my brother Leond of N. York a package of plants collected in the interior and on the western coast of America somewhere about Latt. 46 deg. I am afraid they will be of little value to you. The rain has been so constant where I have been gathering them that they have lost their colors in some cases, and they will be liable to further accident on their route home.
> I shall remain here one more year. You if in Camb. may expect to see me in about one year from the time you receive this. I shall then ask you if you will follow another expedition to this country in pursuit of your science. The cost would be less than living at home.

Among the fifty or so species sent by Wyeth was a large yellow sunflower that Nuttall would designate *Wyethia,* more commonly called Mule's Ears.

His ambition undiminished by his earlier misadventures, Wyeth returned to Boston and raised money for a second trading venture to Oregon. In 1834, he set out from St. Louis again, this time with a party of seventy men, including a band of missionaries and his friend Thomas Nuttall. Upon reaching Oregon in late summer, Wyeth established Fort William on Sauvie Island at the mouth of the Willamette River. There, he planted gardens and began a settlement.

Wyeth's grand scheme was to process salmon and ship it around Cape Horn to eastern markets. But the fish was not properly preserved and had to be tossed overboard along the way. Attempts to grow tobacco and grain for profit were similarly disappointing. For two years, Wyeth's wife waited back in Cambridge for a letter saying that she should join him in Oregon. Instead, she finally received word that he was in "commercial distress" and would be coming home within the year. Wyeth wrote to her:

> *Keep up your spirits, my dear wife, for I expect when I come home, to stop there. Although I shall be poor, yet we can always live. I hope to find my trees growing when I come, and all things comfortable.*

Nathaniel Wyeth did not find fortune in the West, but he is considered the "pioneer of pioneers" in Oregon. His overland expeditions blazed the route that soon would be known as the Oregon Trail. His activities in Oregon also strengthened American claims to that lush region. Though not a scientist himself, Wyeth made a lasting contribution to botany by urging Thomas Nuttall to join him on the 1834 expedition. For the next few years, Nuttall wandered from Oregon to Hawaii to California, seemingly finding plants new to science at every turn.

Mule's Ears, *Wyethia helenioides*

A perennial plant forming a large clump, the basal leaves 1 to 2 feet long and 4 to 6 inches wide—hence the common name Mule's Ears. Small, deep yellow sunflowerlike blooms. Common in grassy fields in the Sierra Nevada foothills, California's Central Valley, and in the California Coast Ranges, from Solano County south to San Luis Obispo County.

Wyethia helenioides

from Childs & Inman's Press.

Wm Darlington M. D.

William Darlington
1782–1863

William D. Brackenridge
1810–1893

A tombstone in West Chester, Pennsylvania, an old town near Philadelphia, is engraved with the outline of a California Cobra Plant. Here lies "large-minded Darlington," wrote an admirer, "who sowed the seeds of public good by lofty word and deed." In the tradition of Benjamin Franklin and Thomas Jefferson, this good doctor energetically threw himself into the needs of his community with an influence so wide that his name was commemorated in the plant world.

In his memoirs, William Darlington wrote of his decision to pursue a medical career:

> *Before I was eighteen I had conceived such an aversion to the uninteresting drudgery of the farm, and felt such a desire to engage in some kind of study of scientific pursuit, that my father consented to let me study medicine . . . on account of its connection with the most interesting natural sciences.*

At the University of Pennsylvania, he studied medicine for the requisite two years under Dr. Benjamin Rush and botany under Professor Benjamin Smith Barton of the Philadelphia Academy of Sciences.

Darlington went on to practice medicine for thirty-four years. In addition, he added significantly to the infrastructure of his community by serving three terms in Congress; by working as the president of the local bank for more than three decades; by establishing medical, agricultural, and horticultural societies; and by participating in the development of a railroad and canal system. Darlington believed so fervently in the American cause in the War of 1812 that he enlisted as an infantry officer, for which he was subsequently cast out of the Society of Friends.

Somehow, amidst all this activity, Darlington found time to study plants. A contemporary botanist once wrote of the doctor that "Botany . . . was only the side issue, the recreation of his life." Still, he used such time as was available for "recreation" to produce a clear and accurate flora of the Chester environs.

Darlington's contributions came to the attention of the eminent botanist John Torrey, who praised him for having "contributed so largely to the scientific reputation of our country." When a strange new member of the Pitcher Plant Family was sent to Torrey by the

William D. Brackenridge

collector William Brackenridge, the botanist named the plant *Darlingtonia californica* after the tireless West Chester doctor.

William Brackenridge, like David Douglas, began his career as a Scottish gardener. In 1838, he joined the worldwide sailing expedition headed by naval captain Charles Wilkes as its assistant botanist. The Wilkes Expedition landed in Oregon in October of 1841. After more than two years at sea, several members, including Brackenridge, welcomed the opportunity to explore the West Coast by hiking overland to Yerba Buena on San Francisco Bay.

One day, as Brackenridge was exploring a small tributary of the headwaters of the Sacramento River near Mount Shasta, or "Snowy Mountain," he met a group of unfriendly Indians. While beating a hasty retreat, he had time only to grab a handful of a strange-looking plant. In his diary, the botanist described his specimen thus: "Leaves 3 ft. long—flower stem exceeding the leaves in length, hab. wet places." From this note, Brackenridge is still remembered as an early botanical collector in northern California.

Due to the lateness of the year, the flowers had passed and not a seed was included in the specimen Brackenridge shipped back East. Nonetheless, when his collection reached New York, Dr. Torrey had no trouble determining that Brackenridge's odd find was new to science based on the leaves alone.

Thus, the *Darlingtonia californica,* or Cobra Plant, provides one of those strange links between the settled East and the wild West. Darlington, the patriot of the East, whose home was closer to the Atlantic Ocean than his namesake plant was to the Pacific, never traveled west, never saw a living specimen of the plant named for him, and never met its discoverer Brackenridge. Still, he must have been intensely proud of the honor done him by Dr. Torrey to have chosen the image of the Cobra Plant to grace his grave for posterity.

Cobra Plant, *Darlingtonia californica*

Two-foot-tall member of the Pitcher Plant Family. Leaves are modified into tubular pitchers, each with a hood and forked tonguelike projection. Crimson, solitary flowers that never fully open. Found only in northern California and southern Oregon in boggy serpentine soil. On the California Native Plant Society's "watch list" as a potentially endangered species.

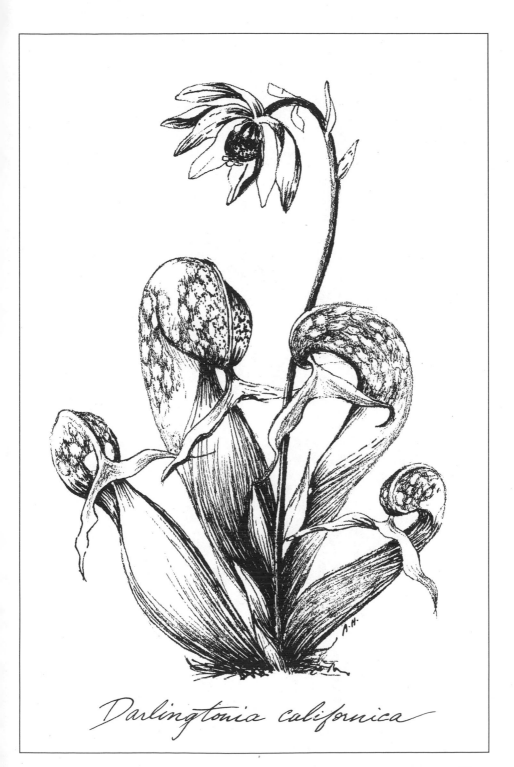

Darlingtonia californica

Asa Gray

Asa Gray
1810–1888

As I write these words in Harvard's Gray Herbarium, a portrait of bearded Professor Asa Gray stares down at me. In a nearby glass case reside the tools of his trade—a small lens, his digger, and his vasculum, or carrying case. On this campus, in the mid-nineteenth century, Dr. Gray established himself as America's preeminent botanical scientist.

Prodigious. Demanding. Indefatigable. Clearness of intellectual vision. A just and genial critic. Such were the words and phrases used by Gray's peers to describe this towering figure. A list of Gray's books and articles contains some 1,100 entries. More than ten thousand letters to Gray have been preserved from six hundred correspondents, including the illustrious botanists John Torrey and George Engelmann and such famous naturalists as Charles Darwin and John Muir.

Gray was an international networker in the finest sense. He traveled to Europe and brought home exciting new ideas. In return, he shipped newly described American plants to colleagues across the Atlantic. While working on his book the *Origin of Species,* Darwin wrote Gray from England asking for a list of American alpine plants. Gray responded not only with the list of plants, but also with an analysis of their distribution throughout North America, Europe, and Japan.

Early in his career, Gray set himself the goal of compiling and describing all known plants of the United States, a monumental undertaking that even he could not complete, despite his long life. In pursuit of this goal, he sought out adventurous collectors to send west and supported their work by scaring up expense money and by helping them sell their specimens. In his later years, scores of collectors who knew of his receptivity sent Gray their specimens for identifying and naming. No wonder his letters at times contain the complaint of the person who has far too much to do.

From the plants sent to him by field collectors, such as Augustus Fendler and Charles Wright, Gray worked out many of the details of botany as it is studied today. His broad knowledge of plants from many environments led him to conclude that their distribution was dependent upon "fitness of climate as to heat and dryness." This insight, in turn, led to his early acceptance of Darwin's revolutionary idea that plants could evolve into varieties, rather than necessarily being "distinct creations."

Who was this man of such prodigious talent and energy? Asa Gray grew up in the rolling hills of upstate New York and began collecting flowers as a teenager. He acquired the title "doctor" upon completion of the medical studies urged on him by his father. A package of plants Gray sent to Dr. Torrey was so well received that the young doctor was taken on as Torrey's lab assistant. The two scientists quickly became friends and colleagues, beginning a lifelong collaboration that resulted in their comprehensive volumes on the flora of the United States. One critic has described these works as "masterpieces of clear and concise arrangement, and of compactness and beauty of method, [which] display great learning and analytical power." In 1842, Gray joined the faculty of Harvard College to teach courses in natural history and to oversee its botanical garden. His academic career precluded his being anything but a tourist collector in the field.

For a man of such stature, it seems ironic that the Spiny Hop Sage, *Grayia spinosa,* is the western genus that bears his name. He received this honor as a young man, while visiting Britain's leading botanist, William Hooker, in Glasgow. Hooker selected a pigweed that had been collected by a British fur trader near the Snake River to call *Grayia.* Gray wrote home, "I am quite content with a Pigweed, and this is a very queer one."

In addition to the *Grayia spinosa,* a peak in the Rocky Mountains memorializes America's best-known botanist. A local mountain man, with a local's provincial view, was once heard to say of the naming of Gray's Peak:

> *Gray, he was a great weed-sharp, down East somewhar, and he gin so many names to this yer bunch-grass and stuff that they thought they'd gin his name to the highest peak, though I don't see it myself.*

For those who know botany, however, the honor seems most appropriate. As one of Gray's admirers put it, "Never again will a single person dominate American botany as Asa Gray held dominion for fifty years."

Spiny Hop Sage, *Grayia spinosa*

A small, common shrub with inconspicuous flowers but conspicuous rose-purple, winged fruits. The leaves are thickish and somewhat pinkish on twigs ending in spinelike tips. Common in desert areas, from southeastern California to eastern Washington, Wyoming, Colorado, and the Great Basin. A good browse plant.

Grayia spinosa

Charles Sargent, "Skinner", and George Engelmann

George Engelmann
1809–1884

George Engelmann personifies the bright, educated immigrant who brings success to himself and to his adopted land. When this young German doctor decided to set up a medical practice in St. Louis on the western edge of the Mississippi, he could not have dreamed that he would be remembered as one of the preeminent botanical scientists of nineteenth-century America.

Quite possibly, Engelmann was the most classically educated scientist in America, having studied at three German universities. After coming to the United States, he spent three years wandering through the Midwest, an area he found rife with new and interesting plants. At first, Engelmann sent his specimens back to European centers of learning for study. It was in Europe that Harvard professor Asa Gray first learned of the doctor's collecting work. By 1840, the two had begun a correspondence and a friendship that lasted until Engelmann's death more than four decades later.

Engelmann had an enviable ability to "timeshare" between his medical and botanical activities. Often, he would work on describing a flower between the arrival of patients. By marshaling his mental and physical resources, he was able to stay active in both fields throughout his lifetime, telling his son, "I would rather die in harness than rust out."

Engelmann's contributions to botany were enormous. In addition to organizing his own 100,000 botanical specimens and writing volumes of technical descriptions, he became the major conduit between field collectors in the West and professors Torrey and Gray in the East. In the frontier outpost of St. Louis, Engelmann sought out fellow Germans, such as Augustus Fendler, to venture into the little-traveled western regions. To support their efforts, he often donated drying paper, promised to find purchasers for their myriad specimens, and even loaned them money. One of Engelmann's many visitors was John C. Frémont, who came to the expert to learn a little about botanical collecting before beginning his western explorations.

Though his many professional and civic responsibilities tied Dr. Engelmann to St. Louis, he and his wife did take trips through the West. They once joined Dr. and Mrs. Charles C. Parry in Colorado, where they were turned back from climbing Parry's Peak by an unseasonable snowstorm. The Engelmanns also went botanizing with Jane and Asa Gray in the Valley of Virginia.

Three years after this happy trip, Mrs. Engelmann died. The doctor was devastated. Only through the efforts of his good friends did he manage to pull himself together. He visited the Grays at Harvard, returning "happy and sad." After that, he was persuaded by

Professor Charles Sprague Sargent and Dr. Parry to join them on a trip to California and the Pacific Northwest to study forest resources.

Today, Dr. Engelmann is remembered in the names of a spruce, a pine, and numerous desert plants. Because many of his collectors trekked across the arid expanses of Texas and New Mexico, Engelmann became personally enamored of such desert plants as the cactus, yucca, and agave. Knowing this, Parry named an agave after him, writing to his friend that "I am anxious to hear what you make of my . . . nice pot plant, [which] grows in dry rock crevices [that I] called *Agave Engelmannii.*"

Engelmann's most enduring legacy came from his connection with Henry Shaw, a wealthy English merchant who resided in St. Louis and dreamed of creating a public garden of the stature of Kew Gardens in London. Shaw contacted Asa Gray and William Hooker for advice and must have been told, "You have a world-class botanist right in your own midst." From this association came Shaw's Garden, now known around the world as the prestigious Missouri Botanical Garden.

Hedgehog Cactus, *Echinocereus Engelmannii*

A mounding cactus forming open-to-dense clumps up to 2 feet high and 3 feet across. Numerous purple, magenta, or lavender flowers. Each spine cluster has four stout, central stalks. Common in southwestern California, southern Nevada, and western and southern Arizona.

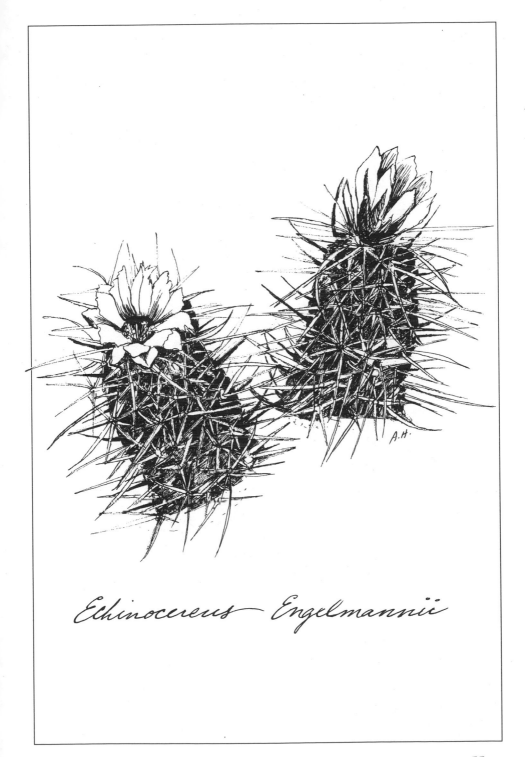

Echinocereus Engelmannii

John C. Frémont

John C. Frémont remains one of the most enigmatic heroes in American history. To his admirers, he was a skilled, even brilliant, engineer, topographer, and expedition leader, as well as a courageous explorer. To his detractors, Frémont was a reckless self-promoter who would do anything to further his political ambitions, even to the point of risking men's lives by ordering foolhardy winter forays across the Sierra Nevada in near-blizzard conditions.

John Frémont's career until he was forty was spent with the Army Corps of Topographical Engineers. He headed five expeditions into the West between 1842 and 1853, fulfilling his youthful dream of participating in "the opening up of unknown lands." While he was best known for his pathfinding and cartography, Frémont had an intense interest in all the sciences, taking special delight in meteorological observations. He once wrote of his passion for exploring that "learning at first hand from Nature herself, the drinking first at her unknown springs, became a source of never-ending delight to me."

Frémont was also a conscientious, though little-trained, botanist. Professors Torrey and Gray were excited about the choice of this bright young man to lead a mapping expedition across the Rocky Mountains in 1842. Gray wrote to his colleague that Lieutenant Frémont must be "indoctrinated" in plant collection and, if successful, would have the 999th Senecio (a genus of widely distributed composite plants) named after him. Before starting out, Frémont went through a quick training stint in St. Louis with George Engelmann, who taught him how to dry and preserve his specimens.

Frémont's unforgettable story is intertwined with that of his intelligent and devoted wife, Jessie, daughter of the expansionist senator from Missouri, Thomas Hart Benton. The interplay between the Bentons and Frémont is told in Irving Stone's novel *Immortal Wife*. Jessie helped her husband take the field notes from his several exploring trips and turn them into widely read memoirs that excited the folks back East about the bounty and beauty of the West. The success of Frémont's narratives surprised them both. Jessie once wrote to her husband that "as far as your report, its popularity astonished even me, your most confirmed and oldest worshipper."

One reason these books were so well received was Frémont's poetic way with words. His works contained evocative descriptions of western landscapes, such as this passage painting a vivid picture of spring wildflowers in an as yet undisturbed southern California:

> *We continued on through a succession of valleys, and came into a most beautiful spot of flower fields; instead of green, the hills*

were purple and orange, with unbroken beds, into which each color was separately gathered. A pale straw color, with a bright yellow, the rich red-orange of the poppy mingled with fields of purple, covered the spot with a floral beauty.

Frémont left a trail of contributions to geography. He was the first to realize the immensity of the Great Basin and to give this vast region its name. "The whole idea of such a desert," he noted, "is a novelty in our country." He also named the break in the coastline near San Francisco the Golden Gate. Today, the explorer's name graces several western towns, while a tall peak he once climbed in the Wind River Range of Wyoming continues to be called Fremont Peak.

He also is remembered for his contributions to botany. A fossil fern found in the careful collection of rocks Frémont sent to a New York geologist bears his name. A tree he called the Sweet Cottonwood, because his animals browsed on the edible inner bark, is now known as the Fremont Cottonwood. And along the freeways of California, you may see the yellow-flowering Fremontia, one of the ten species Frémont discovered in the Golden State.

Fremontia, *Fremontodendron californicum*

A beautiful evergreen shrub or small tree with rough, dark green leaves and large, bright yellow or orangish flowers that bloom in May. Grows on 3,000- to 6,000-foot slopes in chaparral and Yellow Pine areas, from Mount Shasta south through the Sierra Nevada into San Diego County and parts of Arizona. Well adapted to dry areas, shedding leaves in periods of severe drought and then sprouting new ones when rains come. Used frequently in cultivation. Also known as Flannel Bush.

Fremontodendron californicum

Josiah Gregg

Josiah Gregg
1806–1850

"He fell from his horse and died without speaking—died of starvation." Thus ended the life of Josiah Gregg—a wanderer of the western frontier—as reported by his traveling companion L. K. Wood.

Gregg was the self-educated son of pioneer farmers. An omnivorous reader, who taught himself everything from French to cartography, he much preferred the frontier life to dealing with eastern "elegancies." Ever in poor health and always on the move, Gregg tested (and found wanting) the professions of schoolmaster, lawyer, surveyor, trader, and doctor.

Well into his thirties, Gregg settled on exploring and writing as his "career." In 1844, he published a substantial book, still in print, about his years as a western entrepreneur. Its title tells all: *Commerce of the Prairies or the Journal of a Santa Fe Trader During Eight Expeditions Across the Great Western Prairies and a Residence of Nearly Nine Years in Northern New Mexico.* Inside are chapters with such intriguing titles as "Wild Tribes," "Absence of Navigable Streams," "The Mirage, or False Ponds," and "Indifference on the Subject of Horse-breeding."

Looking for his next "wild roam," Gregg joined the Arkansas volunteers as they headed off to war in Mexico in 1846. The soldiers laughed uproariously at their odd companion's mode of travel. One described him as sitting upright on his mule, "wearing his habitual expression of disdainful interest, and holding over his head a red silk parasol."

Gregg was neither a trained nor an experienced botanist when he began his Mexican journey. Only recently had he begun to collect plants and send them to Dr. Engelmann in St. Louis for study. As a novice collector, Gregg was not very sure of his new skills, commenting in a letter to his mentor that his specimens seemed "very badly handled." Still, he was eager to know which of the several hundred specimens he had sent Engelmann were new to science, adding on a sadly prophetic note that he hoped to incorporate their descriptions into his writings "within about a year—if nothing happens."

Engelmann, for his part, was most appreciative of being sent plants from unexplored areas of the Southwest, especially at no cost to himself. In one published report, the doctor wrote that he had been "materially aided by having it in my power to compare" Gregg's specimens with those sent by another collector.

In 1849, Gregg left Mexico for the northwestern corner of California, where he hoped to find gold and, perhaps, to found a new town. His small party endured a wet and foggy winter trapped in a "prison forest" of giant fallen redwood trees. By spring, the gold seekers' ammunition and food were running dangerously low. They were making their way back to civilization when Gregg met his untimely end.

It seems unlikely that Gregg's passing was deeply mourned by his fellow adventurers. According to L. K. Wood, he was hardly a genial traveling companion. Since childhood, Gregg had been a loner, a temperate and serious soul with an investigative mind. To those with whom he traveled, however, he came across as a pesky, intellectual crank. Wood wrote that Gregg looked upon himself as a naturalist and upon his fellows as "ignorant people, who are wholly unable to comprehend the utility of [my] collection."

Wood described an incident that captured this tension perfectly. Gregg had lagged behind the group to measure the circumference of some redwood trees, along with their latitude and longitude, "for the benefit of those who might hereafter visit the spot." His exhausted companions threatened to leave him behind and finally pushed their Indian canoes into a rain-swollen river without him. Wading out after them, "the aged doctor" came aboard spouting "the most withering and violent abuse." Wood concluded his tale by noting, "This stream in commemoration of the difficulty I have just related, we called Mad River." And so it remains today—yet another memento of a plant collector's tribulations.

Catclaw Acacia, *Acacia Greggii*

A very spiny, deciduous small tree or shrub. Light green compound leaves hide small hooked spines with painfully sharp points. Flowers look like bright yellow fuzzy balls. Grows in desert areas from Texas to California and into Mexico, often in thickets along streams. Abundant along the Colorado River through the Grand Canyon.

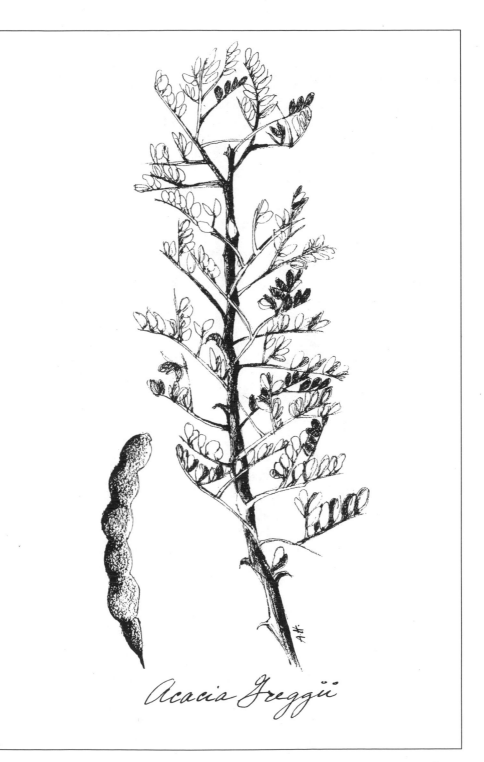

Acacia Greggii

A. Fendler

1861.

Augustus Fendler
1813–1883

During the 1840s, Professor Asa Gray, comfortably situated at Harvard, waited in vain for word of someone to send him plants from the high peaks of the Sangre de Cristo Range at the southern end of the Rockies. The outbreak of war between Mexico and the United States in 1846 created an unexpected opportunity for Gray to acquire his specimens. Upon learning that an army was being organized to conquer New Mexico and California, Gray wrote to his friend George Engelmann:

> *We must have a collector for plants living and dry to go to Santa Fe with the Government Expedition. If I were not so tied up, I would go myself. Have you some good fellow you can send?*

That "good fellow" turned out to be a shy, itinerant tradesman-turned-plant collector named Augustus Fendler.

Fendler was an unlikely choice for such an assignment. He was a solitary man who found in his lonely Thoreau-like existence "a satisfaction of inward peace of mind and bliss higher than expected." Engelmann, however, did not have time to be choosy. When Fendler showed up in St. Louis in 1846 with plants for him to identify, the doctor decided he was just the man Gray was looking for. Gray secured permission for Fendler to join the second contingent of American soldiers heading west to Santa Fe that year. The professor also arranged for his Boston friends to contribute a little expense money to the collector, while Engelmann provided drying paper and a loan of $100.

Fendler reached Santa Fe at the end of September, several weeks after New Mexico had been forced to accept American domination. Gray later commented that the collector was "disagreeably surprised by the apparent sterility of the region where his researches were to commence in the following season." These initial misgivings vanished once Fendler set to work. Over the following year, he collected more than a thousand specimens in the Santa Fe region.

Few of these plants were from the high-alpine areas of the Sangre de Cristo Range that Gray had so hoped to see explored. Fendler's situation was just not propitious for high-altitude collecting. Spring doesn't reach the high country until June or July, and by that time, he was getting ready to leave New Mexico. In addition, mountain travel was particularly risky that year. The Ute, Apache, and Navajo were on the warpath, making venturing into the wilderness unsafe. Many Mexican settlers in the region also resented the intrusion of the Americans. While Fendler was living in Santa Fe, the first American governor of New Mexico was killed in nearby Taos, and his scalp was paraded around the plaza. So perhaps it is no wonder that Fendler seldom collected more than a day's walk from town.

Living in Santa Fe was expensive then, as now. The presence of American troops drove up prices for everything. Fendler was forced to sell his watch and gun to raise funds for his return to St. Louis, where he hoped to be recompensed for his losses. As this letter to Gray reveals, he was sorely disappointed.

> *When my pecuniary means at Santa Fe were nearly all exhausted, when I had to sacrifice one thing after another of my most necessary effects, to keep up a few days longer the scanty support of our lives, in order to collect something more of the vegetation of that region: I looked forward with the utmost confidence to those gentlemen in the East, who had induced me to go out to Santa Fe, and who would as I hoped, leave me not without assistance as soon as I should have returned with my collections in St. Louis. It was this hope that made me bear all the difficulties most cheerfully under the happy impression that the enjoyment of the fruits of my labour would soon compensate for all. But alas! It was to be otherwise.*

Back in St. Louis, Fendler was helped by Dr. Engelmann to sort his plants into families and then send them on to Gray. The professor wrote that the specimens were "perfectly charming! So well made, so full and perfect. Better were never made." Gray went on to publish a famous paper titled "Plantae Fendlerianae Novi-Mexicanae," in which he reached important conclusions about plant distribution.

After his adventure in New Mexico, Fendler's life went from one tragedy to another, ending in his death while traveling in Latin America. Despite his many troubles, however, one hopes that he took some pride in knowing that his name was preserved in the names of a multitude of southwestern plants.

Yerba Desierto, *Fendlerella utahensis*

A low shrub with numerous small, opposite leaves and clusters of inconspicuous, white flowers blooming June to August. Grows in rocky canyons and open pine woods of the Southwest, from western Texas to southern California and south into Mexico. Common around the Grand Canyon.

Fendlerella utahensis

Charles Wright

Charles Wright
1811–1885

You wrote to me of working like a dog. I know how you live—then call your situation dog-paradise and mine hog- and ass-paradise combined and you may realize my situation—sleep all night if you can in the rain and walk 12-15 miles next day in the mud and then overhaul a huge package of soaked plants and dry them by the heat of the clouds.

This blunt complaint to Asa Gray from Charles Wright, one of his most trusted collectors, sums up a symbiotic relationship that endured for forty years. Gray, the demanding, urbane academic, once summed up his faithful correspondent by commenting:

You do not know what a helpless odd fellow he is—good for nothing but to collect and dry specimens—but one of the most unselfish & good-natured men I know.

Both men benefited from their long friendship. Wright found the career of his choosing working as "Gray's collector." In that capacity, he spent eight years botanizing in Texas, joined an around-the-world scientific expedition, and collected for eleven years in Cuba. Gray, in turn, obtained new specimens that helped expand his understanding of plant distribution. To make this relationship work, however, the busy professor had to put himself out to meet Wright's needs, purchasing books and supplies in Boston and sending them to wherever the collector was working. And never could Gray write enough letters to keep the lonely Wright happy.

Charles Wright grew up in the Connecticut village of Wethersfield. He attended Yale, where he spent his time hiking, in part to avoid the college's literary clubs with their requisite public speaking. After graduation, Wright headed to Texas, where he taught school and worked as a surveyor. In 1844, he began sending plants to Gray, who saw great potential in having Wright work as his personal collector.

Eager to extend the work of Ferdinand Lindheimer, one of the earliest collectors in eastern Texas, and to fill in the gaps of Augustus Fendler's New Mexico collection, Gray obtained passage for Wright with an army supply train heading across western Texas. Wright was less than pleased with the arrangement. The officers in charge of the expedition as much as ignored him, forcing the collector to walk the nearly seven hundred miles from San Antonio to El Paso, with only his trunk and drying papers riding in the supply wagon. Still, with his eyes close to the ground, Wright could all the better spy the small flowering desert plants.

In 1851, Wright joined the Mexican Boundary Survey, a federal expedition charged with settling the location of America's new southern border after the conclusion of the Mexican War. With the inclusion of engineers, zoologists, geologists, and several botanists in the surveying party, the expedition was "a kind of a graduate school for collectors." They found the arid lands of the Chihuahuan and Sonoran deserts dotted with Ocotillo, Palo Verde, Mesquite, Saltbush, and numerous cacti. Wright helped collect many of the 2,600 species that were sent east to Professor John Torrey for description.

Wright's work in Texas and with the Mexican Boundary Survey helped to open up the Southwest botanically and to document the vast differences between the flora of the eastern woodlands and central plains and that of the southwestern desert. Asa Gray based his "Plantae Wrightianae Texano-Neo-Mexicanae," the first botanical work published by the Smithsonian Institution, on Wright's collections. In further recognition of Wright's contributions, George Engelmann, the cactus enthusiast, described one of his new species as *Opuntia Wrightii,* saying that the name "is forever inseparably connected with the botany of our southern Boundary."

In the last decade of his life, Wright returned to the village of his youth to live with his two unmarried sisters and an invalid brother. One summer day, he simply did not return from his routine of evening chores. His sisters found his body lying on the ground in a state of peaceful repose.

Wright's Verbena, *Verbena Wrightii*

A flowering plant with many branching, erect stems up to 30 inches high. Leaves are deeply divided. Rosy-purple flower appears on a sticky, glandular calyx. Blooms from April to October. Common in western Texas and Colorado and across New Mexico. Rare in eastern Arizona.

Verbena Wrightii

Albert Kellogg

Albert Kellogg
1813–1887

Albert Kellogg was of one of many "forty-niners" whose hopes of filling their pockets with California gold ended in disappointment. Even so, this genial bachelor doctor stayed on in California to play a leading role in the development of science in the Golden State.

Kellogg arrived in Sacramento in the summer of 1849, a member of the Connecticut Mining and Trading Company. What he found was a gold rush that had already peaked. For most miners, digging in streambeds was laborious and unrewarding work. Drunkenness and cholera abounded. The little law and order that existed in mining camps was maintained by thrown-together juries, whose members believed in the efficacy of the gallows.

With his dream of a bountiful paradise fading, Kellogg moved to San Francisco and opened a drugstore. Thanks to the efforts of volunteers, the city was just becoming an organized metropolis. Vigilantes policed the streets, and citizen fire brigades responded when wooden buildings caught on fire.

Kellogg, too, found a way to help build this new society. In 1853, he joined four other doctors, a realtor, and the city's school superintendent to create the California Academy of Sciences. As they mapped plans for their new enterprise, the academy's founders were ahead of their time. They resolved that "we highly approve the help of females in every department of natural history and earnestly seek their cooperation." These words were to prove prophetic with the later hiring of Katherine Brandegee and Alice Eastwood as curators for the academy.

Kellogg's energetic devotion to the Academy of Sciences was inspired by his love of botany. One friendly critic noted that Kellogg had a "childlike enthusiasm" for plants and that "though sometimes his comments on botany were in error, they were true so far as he was concerned." Asa Gray, the dean of American botany, described Kellogg as "a good-hearted and impractical fellow," as well as an occasional "nuisance."

The good doctor's enthusiasm for plants reflected his religious beliefs. He was a member of San Francisco's Swedenborgian New Jerusalem Church, which held that God is to be found everywhere in nature and that the physical world is symbolic of the spiritual world. Many of Kellogg's botanical writings reveal an otherworldly ecological mystic, who sought "correspondences" between the natural world and spiritual states. In his notes, for example, he writes of his belief that

Our Lord when a child had divine visions of the infinite beauty

*which clothes all things when the internal and external are
joined in heavenly harmony.*

Kellogg's passion was the careful study of trees. He gave the
name "Washington Cedar" to the gigantic redwood trees of the Sierra
Nevada and then proudly told an English collector, William Lobb, of
their incredible girth and height. Lobb said his polite good-byes,
headed directly to the Sierra, where he collected seeds and two live
trees, and then hurried across the Atlantic.

To the horror of American botanists, an English botanist gave the
name *Wellington gigantea* to the huge trees to commemorate the
Duke of Wellington, "the greatest of modern heroes, [who] stands as
high above his contemporaries as this Californian tree above the
surrounding forests."

Unwilling to let the Europeans have the last word, the California
Academy trustees insisted that the name Washington Cedar must
stand. Today, we know the mountain redwoods as the *Sequoia
gigantea* and, because of their mythic proportions and great age,
often regard these ancient trees as plant-heroes among living things.

After retiring from business, Kellogg turned his full attention to his
favorite trees and shrubs. The botanist Willis Lynn Jepson
remembered visiting the old downtown Academy of Sciences while
he was still a student in the 1880s. There was Kellogg, working "in
his shirt sleeves and his old red flannel waistcoat, making drawings
of twigs." From these careful studies came the four hundred
botanical drawings that illustrate Kellogg's book *West American
Oaks.*

With the "love of a father," Kellogg spent his years nourishing the
little acorn of the academy, helping it to grow into the giant, well-
rooted institution we know today.

California Black Oak, *Quercus Kelloggii*

A large, dark-barked deciduous oak. Big, bright leaves are deeply
cut, each lobe ending in one to three bristle-tipped teeth. Found
between 2,000 and 5,000 feet, from central Oregon through
California's Sierra Nevada and Coast Ranges. Especially notable in
Yosemite Valley.

Quercus Kelloggii

Charles C. Parry

Charles Christopher Parry
1823–1890

Charles C. Parry was a collector of botanists as well as of plants. During his long career, this quiet, gentle scientist became the trusted friend of the major naturalists of his day, including such notables as John Torrey, Asa Gray, George Engelmann, John Muir, Edward L. Green, Edward Palmer, and John G. Lemmon. Parry even named two peaks in the Colorado Rockies for Torrey and Gray, and in 1872, he personally escorted each professor up the slopes of "his mountain." On two trips to England, Parry's birthplace, he also won the affection and admiration of Sir Joseph Hooker, the director of Kew Gardens.

An itinerary of Parry's botanical rovings reads like a lifelong marathon. He began collecting plants as a young man in New York. Over the next half century, he made collecting forays to Lake Superior, Panama, the Rocky Mountains, Kansas, New Mexico, Arizona, California, Wyoming, Utah, and Mexico. Early in his career, Parry spent three years with the Mexican Boundary Survey, exploring the southwest deserts. Nearly thirty years later, he was still exploring the Southwest, this time as a member of the Pacific Railway Survey. A few weeks before he died in 1890, Parry made a collecting trip to Canada. This record is even more impressive when one considers that during the first half of Parry's collecting career, railroads had not yet been built across the West.

When not on collecting expeditions, Dr. Parry worked as a botanist with the Department of Agriculture in Washington, D.C. Later, he settled in Davenport, Iowa, which Parry considered his home base. But he doesn't seem to have been home much! Perhaps his drive to be constantly on the move stemmed from personal tragedy. At the age of thirty, Parry married. Five years later, his wife died. Parry lost his young daughter as well, while she was still "a fair, unfolding flower." In time he remarried, and the second Mrs. Parry became his companion on his collecting trips and in his study of plants.

Parry was considered a major force in the discovery of many species new to science. However, his documentation of these discoveries, according to contemporary comments, was shoddy and even nonexistent. Parry simply did not have the temperament for writing up descriptions or compiling notes. Torrey, who had been his professor at Columbia, described Parry as

one of the quietest men in the world—He pokes about & turns over any collection of plants that may be lying about, without seeming to have any special object in view. As he puts no information on the labels of his plants I sometimes make him sit down while I extract, little by little, what he knows about particular specimens in his collections.

One of Parry's most beautiful finds was a fragrant yellow lily now known as Parry's Lily. He came across this rare plant in 1876, while hiking through the moist canyons east of Los Angeles in the company of fellow collectors John Gill Lemmon and Edward Palmer. When Parry died fourteen years later, the naturalist John Muir wrote nostalgically about the lilies of the field:

> *It seems as if all the good flower people, at once great and good, have died now that Parry is gone—Torrey, Gray, Kellogg, and Parry. Plenty more botanists left, but none we have like these. Men more amiable apart from their intellectual power I never knew, so perfectly clean and pure they were—pure as lilies, yet tough and unyielding in mental fibre as liveoaks.*

Parry's Lily, *Lilium Parryi*

A rare plant of southern Arizona and California also known as the Lemon Lily. Found along streams at about 6,500 feet. Very showy, fragrant, pale-yellow flowers, usually marked with tiny dark dots.

Lilium Parryi

Edward Palmer with Ipomoea arborescens

Edward Palmer
1831–1911

Little has been written of Edward Palmer, a solitary explorer who collected more than ten thousand plants from Florida, the American Southwest, Mexico, and the islands off Baja California. The unhappy circumstances of his life seem to have left him in the shadow of history.

Palmer was born in England but spent his adult life in the United States. After a brief stint of medical training, he abandoned any plan of becoming a doctor to follow his avocations—botany and ethnography. Not only did he collect thousands of plants, he also studied and recorded the ways of the Kiowa, Apache, Wichita, Yuma, and several native peoples of Mexico.

For some reason, fate seemed determined to make life difficult for Palmer. He returned from his first collecting venture, a journey to Paraguay, to find that his name had been left off the expedition's report. Time after time, his collections went astray. One batch of plants was lost in a shipwreck off the California coast. Many of his specimens disappeared when Palmer entrusted them to less than reliable colleagues for mailing. Still another collection took three years to reach the East Coast, and by then, his findings were no longer new and interesting.

Palmer's personal life was also marked by misfortune. His young English bride died just a few weeks after reaching the United States, a victim of yellow fever. Palmer himself suffered from recurrences of malaria and other debilitating illnesses. The collector seemed to be accident-prone as well. He once injured his spine and, another time, gashed his head falling off a recalcitrant mule.

For most of his long life, Palmer was considered just a private, though prolific, collector by his associates at the Smithsonian Institution and the Department of Agriculture. His most significant scientific contributions were made during the 1870s, when the federal government sent him to the Southwest to study agricultural resources and the ethnobotany of wild plants. From there, Palmer moved on to Mexico, then the newest "hot spot" for collecting. In Mexico, he hooked up with Dr. Charles C. Parry, who wrote of Palmer, perhaps unfairly, that "like all us old *codgers* he knows how to *shirk hard work.*"

While Palmer is little remembered today, his contributions did not go unnoticed during his lifetime. Two hundred species were named for him during his fifty-five years of collecting. Dr. Engelmann named the largest and most common of the agave plants and a Southwest oak for him. Professor Gray called a new genus *Palmerella* in his honor. When the collector turned eighty, the Botanical Society of Washington gave a party to celebrate his accomplishments, an event that brought tears streaming down the old botanist's face.

Palmer died a few months later. In his will, he indicated a desire to have his adventures and discoveries written up for posterity. Instead, his papers and field notes sat neglected on a shelf until 1962. Only then did a new generation of botanists learn something about the collector honored by Gray for his "indefatigable and fruitful explorations . . . to the islands off Lower California, in which region he has accomplished more than all his predecessors."

Scented Penstemon, *Penstemon Palmeri*

A flowering plant growing in clumps up to 4 feet high. Its sweet-smelling, flesh-colored flowers are marked with purple stripes that lead bees to the nectar within the corolla. Found in high deserts, from Idaho south to Arizona and the eastern Mojave of California. Particularly abundant in Bryce and Zion national parks.

Penstemon Palmeri

JG Lemmon. 1894

John Gill Lemmon
1832–1908

Sara Plummer Lemmon
1836–1923

Looking over old plant specimens in Gray's Herbarium at Harvard University, one finds label after label reading "J. G. Lemmon and wife." These simple notes attest to a warm and enduring relationship, as well as a long and productive botanical partnership.

John Lemmon seems to have been born with a love of plants. His mother once said that she believed he had inherited "the reincarnated spirit of an ancient weedpuller." This spirit was almost snuffed out during the Civil War. While fighting for the Union, Lemmon was captured and sent to Andersonville, the infamous Confederate prison where barely one hundred of some five thousand starving prisoners were able to stand unaided upon their release.

After the war, the nervous and exhausted veteran traveled west to recuperate on his brother Frank's farm in the Sierra Nevada foothills. Slowly, Lemmon recovered and began to relate to nature again. He wrote that

As I peered out of the windows, and later groped about the premises, the strange flowers, bushes, and even the trees proclaimed the fact that I was in a practically unknown world.

Lemmon collected some of these unknown plants and sent the specimens to Professor Asa Gray, whom he idolized as "the Father of Botany." Gray cheerfully responded, "You have discovered seven new plants—new to science. Good! Send some more!"

When Lemmon looked over Gray's list of the seven new plants, he was elated to learn that "the curious five-leafed clover, found intruding on Frank's front doorstep, had become (overnight) *Trifolium Lemmoni.*" This scholarly recognition of something that he loved to do had a revitalizing effect on Lemmon. His energy returned, and he went on to live and collect plants for another forty years.

A decade after coming to California, Lemmon met a kindred spirit in Sara Plummer, a fellow member of a Santa Barbara botanical club. Plummer was the proprietress of a small library that she considered "a haven for intellectual development." The two were married in 1880 after a four-year courtship.

For their honeymoon, the Lemmons planned an extended "botanical wedding trip" that took them to Arizona and New Mexico

Sara Plummer Lemmon

in search of the elusive wild potato. While in Arizona, the Lemmons were determined to explore the rugged Santa Catalina Mountains. In the spring of 1881, they ascended the highest peak in that range with the help of E. O. Stratton, a local rancher. Stratton named the peak Mount Lemmon in honor of Sara Lemmon, the first white woman to make that climb. In 1905, on the occasion of their twenty-fifth wedding anniversary, the Lemmons returned to Arizona, found Stratton, and once again the trio climbed Mount Lemmon.

The Lemmons made their home in Oakland, where the sign above their door read, "Lemmon Herbarium." Inside the house one evening, the couple had good cause for botanical exultation. For some time, John Lemmon had been pestering Asa Gray to name something for his wife, and the couple had just received word that the professor had named a new genus *Plummera,* honoring Sara's maiden name. "We have just held a grand celebration," wrote John, "mother & I dancing around the room . . . alternately shouting for joy and weeping with gratitude."

By this time, Professor Gray may have been getting a bit tired of receiving one request after another from the Lemmons to name plants after them. "Why, you have *Lemmonis* as thick as locusts all round!" he was heard to complain. And in truth, such species could be found all over the West.

In their later years, both Lemmons were hired by the California Board of Forestry to use their field experience to help preserve the state's diverse forests. In the words of a contemporary romantic:

Thus hand in hand, shoulder to shoulder, these sweet-spirited, amiable, and devoted heroes have lived and worked, quietly benefiting a people, many of whom were never even aware of their existence.

Lemmon's Paintbrush, *Castilleja Lemmonii*

A perennial, many-stemmed plant with narrow leaves. Flower heads have purple-tipped bracts and sepals. Blooms in July and August. Found in high meadows of the Sierra Nevada, from Lassen to Inyo counties. Especially notable in the meadows near Tioga Pass in Yosemite National Park.

Castilleja
Lemmonii

Rebecca Austin

The wifely chores of pioneer women were life-consuming, but a few of these hardy souls still managed to find time for their own interests. For Rebecca Austin, that interest was botany. John Gill Lemmon was much impressed by this "woman who was cooking for miners and at the same time trying to study nature under such adverse circumstances."

Studying nature under adverse circumstances was nothing new for Rebecca Austin. Growing up in Kentucky, she found that the educational opportunities for women interested in natural science were almost nonexistent. After her parents died, she taught school long enough to earn tuition to an academy in Illinois. There, Rebecca was introduced to Latin and the study of science. After being left a young widow by her first husband, Rebecca married James Austin, who lured his new bride west with stories of California gold.

In 1875, the Austins settled in Butterfly Valley in northern California. Whenever possible, Rebecca packed up her press, hoisted a pick over her shoulder, and headed off for a day of plant collecting. More than once, she "forgot the family dinner" in the delight of making a new find.

On one of these expeditions, Austin encountered the curious *Darlingtonia californica,* or Cobra Plant. This plant had been discovered hurriedly by the Scottish collector William Brackenridge three decades earlier, but Austin was the first person to study it closely and to notice that it did not behave like other plants.

One can imagine this stern-faced woman, hair drawn back severely, standing in a rainstorm observing her serpent look-alikes. She notices that the raindrops are prevented by the hood of the plant from entering its pitcher. From this, she concludes that the fluid trapped inside the leaves must be made by the plant itself.

Or, picture Austin shedding her high-top shoes and wading into a cold bog to feed bits of meat or insects to a Cobra Plant. She observes that while the fluid in the plant's pitcher does not actually digest the food, decomposition nonetheless takes place. Through careful observation, Austin also finds that the age of a Cobra Plant can be determined by its leaf-scars and by the whorls of its rootlets.

To find out more about this strange plant, Austin began corresponding with William Canby, a naturalist from Delaware. In kind response, Canby sent Austin the first hand lens she had ever owned. Canby even paid a visit to Austin in 1878 to see her odd plants.

In his book *Darwiniana,* Asa Gray credited Rebecca Austin with having made "the principal observations upon this pitcher plant."

Such was the fascination of the Cobra Plant that Gray advised his California readers to "take notice, that a small box of roots, delivered alive in Boston, New York or London, would be pecuniarily as valuable as a considerable lump of gold." Had Rebecca Austin heeded Gray's advice, she might indeed have found gold in California's soil!

Phantom Orchid, *Cephalanthera Austinae*

The species name of this strange saprophytic orchid means "ivory plant." Its stout, white stem grows 1 to 3 feet tall from a creeping rootstock and bears from five to twenty tiny white or yellow-tinged flowers. Grows in dry conifer forests under 6,000 feet, from northern California through Washington and Idaho. Typical habitat is in the Sierra Nevada near Quincy, California.

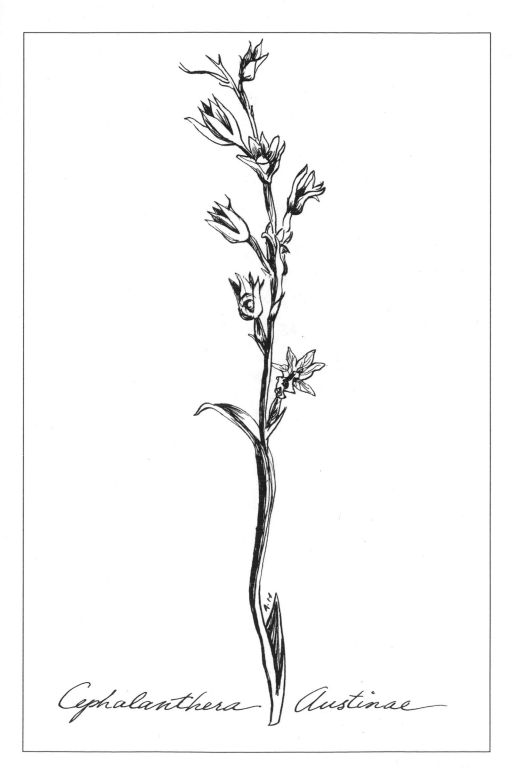

Cephalanthera Austinae

Edward Greene

Edward Lee Greene
1843-1915

Edward L. Greene was a seeker, a controversial crusader, who spent his life in an unending quest for what he considered the truth about God and nature. Perhaps this quest began in childhood when Greene's mother impressed on him the belief that "flowers are a gift from the kind Heavenly Father and all nature is but a revelation of the Divine." Greene grew up to become a botanist, preacher, and ascetic bachelor, who subscribed to a life of poverty—a latter-day St. Francis.

Born into a Baptist family in Rhode Island, Greene served as an Episcopal priest in Colorado, New Mexico, and California. His was never the calm path. He created such controversy at St. Mark's Church in Berkeley, California, that church leaders locked him out. Wearing his cassock and wielding an ax, Greene stormed the church with a band of loyal parishioners, broke down the door, and proceeded to conduct services. By 1886, Greene had turned to Catholicism, which represented to him "a simple and devout recital of how God revealed His truth."

During his ministerial years, Greene spent his spare time collecting plants, and he is given credit for having more field knowledge than any other botanist of his day. Without thought of the consequences, he worked fearlessly to reduce the dominance of the eastern scientific establishment by building up the scientific credibility and independence of botanical researchers in the West. His self-assurance and pride in western scientists led him into many verbal battles with Asa Gray, the academic authority in American botany. He once complained to Gray that

> It is in your power to exalt a man, in the estimation of the scientific public, to very high rank as a botanist [or] you can easily relegate him to the limbo of conceited "cranks." You appear to have decided how you will dispose of me.

Greene's conservative religious faith impeded his acceptance of Darwin's challenging views of evolution. He believed that each species was created by God and could not have variations. Thus, each kind of plant was a separate species. It is said that he would sometimes burn hybrids, believing that they should be eliminated to help keep the world in a state of perfection.

Eventually, Greene left the ministry to become a professor of botany, first at the University of California at Berkeley, where he started the first botanical garden in the West, and later, at the Catholic University of America in the nation's capital. While teaching, he established the journals *Erythea* and *Piittonia*, which he used as platforms for publishing his often controversial views. One of his crusades focused on the naming of plants. Greene believed that plant names should be researched back into history, so each species could be given its earliest name. What confusion could have ensued had he won that battle!

Even today, Greene's quixotic personality attracts both admirers and detractors. To some, he was a fearless investigator; to others, a pest. The botanist Willis Lynn Jepson, who had many dealings with Greene over California plants, perhaps summed him up best when he wrote of Greene's attack on any problem: "He rode at it full-tilt like a medieval knight. The conflict was short, sharp, decisive, and often highly interesting."

Flame Butterweed, *Senecio Greenei*

A low-growing plant, with long-stemmed, roundish leaves forming a basal tuft. Leaves are sometimes reddish, especially at the base. Flower stems hold one to three ragged-appearing flower heads, each with eight to fourteen drooping, orange flowers. Grows in chaparral and on wooded slopes of the northern Coast Ranges of California, usually in serpentine soils.

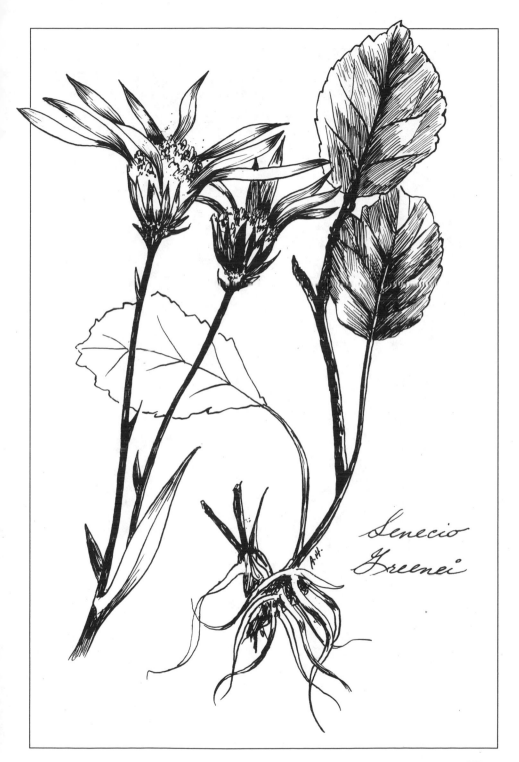

Senecio
Greenei

Thomas Howell

Thomas Howell
1842–1912

The Pacific Northwest was the botanical terrain of Thomas Howell, a regional collector, who, in the judgment of Edward L. Greene, "accomplished the greatest amount of meritorious and valuable scientific work that was ever done by any man of any epoch on so rudimentary an education in letters."

To characterize Howell's formal education as rudimentary borders on understatement. He attended school for a short three months as a teenager. What education the boy did receive came from his father, who had been trained as a doctor. Howell grew up to become a "steady and successful farmer" on Sauvie Island, located near Portland, Oregon, at the confluence of the Willamette and Columbia rivers. Later, he turned the farm over to his brother, Joseph, and took up the trade of grocer.

The Howell farmstead has been preserved as an historic site by the Oregon Historical Society. Today, visitors to Howell Park on Sauvie Island can tour the family's restored home, explore an agricultural museum of nineteenth-century farm implements, and wander through an orchard featuring more than one hundred varieties of apples brought west by pioneer farmers.

In the 1870s, the Howell brothers were both bitten by the botany bug and began collecting local plants. Because they had scant reference materials and lacked access to scientists, they sent at least some of their specimens east to Harvard University for identification. Harvard botanist Asa Gray took note of the Howells' contributions in 1878, when he named a pond plant they had discovered *Howellia aquatilis*. Gray wrote that he had chosen this name to honor "the discoverers, who are assiduous collectors and acute observers . . . who have already much increased the knowledge of the botany of Oregon."

As a collector, Thomas Howell was all too aware that no comprehensive flora of the Pacific Northwest had yet been published. Around 1880, the grocer-turned-botanist decided to fill the gap himself by producing his own *A Flora of Northwest America*. It would be his magnum opus.

Howell's new project proved to be an enormous undertaking. Collecting specimens and getting them identified and described was challenge enough. Once armed with his plant descriptions, however, Howell found that he could not afford to hire a good printer to set botanical type. He surmounted this problem by obtaining lead type and learning how to set text at home, eight pages at a time. No doubt Howell improved his spelling in the process! When finished with a section, the botanist-turned-typesetter toted his boxes of type to Portland for printing.

A Flora of Northwest America evolved section by section until, at last, Howell published the complete book under one cover in 1903. The finished work covered nearly eight hundred pages with a twenty-four-page index. It contained descriptions of more than three thousand species, some sixty of them new to science. Howell's book gained quick acceptance as a major reference work on the flora of Oregon, Washington, and Idaho, and remains, even today, a monument to its creator's unstinting toil and sacrifice.

Howellia, *Howellia aquatilis*

An annual aquatic plant with very slender stems and leaves. Tiny flowers appear from May to August, some of which have whitish or lavender petals and others no petals at all. This member of the Bluebell Family is found in ponds throughout Washington, Idaho, and Oregon's Willamette Valley.

Howellia aquatilis

Townshend and Katherine Brandegee

Townshend Brandegee
1843-1925

Katherine Layne Curran Brandegee
1844-1920

"Brandegee should have been born a woman and Mrs. Brandegee should have been a man," commented Marcus Jones, a fellow plant collector who admired them both. Townshend Brandegee was a "little, quiet, refined man," who, before marrying at age forty-six, was known as "a great friend of the ladies, and a hard student, an old bachelor." In contrast, Jones found Katherine Brandegee to be "the most virile woman I ever knew." She was a robust woman, careless of her dress, who enjoyed a beer and who would take off for weeks at a time to go collecting by herself or with a packer.

Townshend Brandegee was a Connecticut Yankee who first tasted adventure during the Civil War. Later, he would refer with some humor to the final days of that awesome conflict as the time that "Gen. Grant and I took Richmond."

After the war, Brandegee enrolled in Yale University, where he earned a degree in civil engineering. While at Yale, he studied with Professor William Brewer, who had recently returned from a survey expedition to California. No doubt Brewer regaled his students with many of the tales that would later appear in his journal of the expedition, *Up and Down California in 1860-1864.*

Once graduated, Brandegee headed for Colorado and New Mexico and put his engineering skills to work in railroad construction. Since construction workers were paid by the month, they refused to work on Sundays. This gave Brandegee time to develop his interest in botany. He used his free days to explore the high mountain meadows of the San Juan and Wasatch ranges, collecting plants to his heart's content.

Professor Asa Gray heard of the young engineer's botanical efforts and recommended him for a post with the U.S. Geological and Geographical Survey, headed by the nation's eminent geologist, Ferdinand Hayden. Brandegee accepted the job of assistant topographer and botanical collector with the Hayden expedition to southwest Colorado in 1875. From Colorado, he moved farther west to collect plants on the islands bordering southern California. By 1888, Brandegee had settled in California and was focusing his collecting activity on Mexico's Baja Peninsula.

It was through his association with the California Academy of Sciences that Townshend Brandegee met Katherine Layne Curran, the academy's curator of botany and his future wife. A California native, Katherine was one of the first women to graduate from medical school in that state. When patients were not forthcoming, she turned to the study of plants and became one of the important botanists of her day. Katherine was known for her ability to make careful and intelligent discriminations among plants. Her sharp pen and incisive mind made strong and favorable impressions on such collectors and botanists as Marcus Jones and E. L. Greene.

Townshend and Katherine were married in 1889. Their honeymoon was pedestrian—they walked and botanized from San Diego to San Francisco. For a few years, they lived in San Diego in a house described by one visitor as perched "high on the mesa above the town, with a brick building to house their herbarium and a small but well-stocked botanical garden."

After their marriage, the Brandegees founded and, for nearly two decades, funded the botanical journal *Zoe*. Many of Katherine's criticisms, both destructive and constructive, appear there. According to a contemporary, she was a straight shooter who believed "in public reproof of errors and attitudes of mind contrary to her own idea of scientific accuracy and method." Such attitudes fostered respect, not love, in the scientific community, but her marriage with her little engineer endured for three decades.

The Brandegees spent their later years at the University of California at Berkeley, where Townshend was appointed honorary curator of the school's herbarium. They also donated their large botanical library and collection of plant specimens to the university. These gifts remain a lasting tribute to this botanical odd couple, who, both together and separately, collected plants throughout California, Baja California, and western Nevada.

Greenhorn Fritillary, *Fritillaria Brandegei*

A rare plant with four to eight leaves growing in whorls on lower stems. Upper leaves are small and alternate. Small, nodding, but wide-open flowers vary from greenish yellow to reddish purple, becoming lighter in color near the edges and on the backsides. Grows in granitic soil in California's Sierra Nevada.

Fritillaria Brandegei

Alice Eastwood by her touring car "Leucy"

Alice Eastwood
1855–1953

Heroine Lowers Priceless Specimens
TO SAFETY IN HER APRON

So might the *San Francisco Chronicle* have headlined a story about the selfless actions of Alice Eastwood, botanical curator for the California Academy of Sciences, after the 1906 earthquake. Soon after the sides of the San Andreas Fault lurched past one another, fires fed by leaking gas pipes began to ravage San Francisco. Realizing that the academy would soon be engulfed in flames, Eastwood climbed the banister next to a collapsed marble staircase and rescued nearly 1,500 type specimens (the specimens used by botanists to define a species or lesser group). These priceless treasures represented fifty-three years of California collecting.

Alice Eastwood was born in Ontario, Canada. Following the death of her mother, she lived with her uncle, a country doctor who sparked her interest in flowers. Alice later joined her brother and father in Colorado. Forced to drop out of high school for lack of funds, she studied on her own and graduated with honors. The self-taught scholar became a teacher in the town of Kiowa, Colorado, where she turned her charges into little naturalists. At the same time, she began teaching herself botany using Asa Gray's *Manual*. By the time Eastwood left Colorado, she had become a respected collector. More than a dozen plants native to that state bear her name.

Eastwood moved to San Francisco in 1892 and, within a year, succeeded Katherine Brandegee as curator of botany for the California Academy of Sciences. She remained in that post for more than five decades, finally leaving at her own request when she turned ninety. On her retirement, Eastwood received many tributes, including the naming of a redwood grove in northern California in her honor.

Throughout her long career, Eastwood was known for her delightful botanical prose, such as this description of the poppy:

> *The* Eschscholzia *so glows with the sunbeams caught in its chalice that it diffuses light upon the other flowers and the grass. This poppy will not shine unless the sun beams on it, but folds itself up and goes to sleep.*

Eastwood's hiking companions on Mount Tamalpais used equally vivid images to describe the lady curator. One remembered her as

> *a hatless, short-skirted, broad-shouldered woman of wonderful strength—who used to trudge easily 20 miles a day with the sun*

in her serene bronze face and the wind in her flying hair,
carrying her heavy plant presses on her back.

In the 1930s and 1940s, Eastwood formed a team with her assistant, John Thomas Howell, who was himself a recognized botanist and succeeded her as curator. The two began the journal *Leaflets of Western Botany*. They also traveled around the western states in a voluminous touring car nicknamed Leucy, after a plant, of course. Howell wrote of their excursions:

> *On our field trips Miss Eastwood occupied the back seat of the car and from there directed the procedure of the expedition and took care of pressing the plants. We would drive along slowly until some plant would attract us and we would then stop. If the location proved particularly favorable, Miss Eastwood would collect in the vicinity of the car while I would go farther away in search of other plants. On our trips I was always more interested in collecting intensively in a restricted area; Miss Eastwood desired to collect extensively over more territory: if only we could stop longer, I was certain I would discover another treasure; Miss Eastwood was just as certain that the treasure was up the road and around the next bend. So we did well together: Eastwood and Howell covered much ground intensively!*

During her first year in California, while hiking in the blistering summer heat of the San Joaquin Valley, Eastwood came upon a new sunflower. Townshend Brandegee named the genus *Eastwoodia*. When Eastwood turned eighty, a speechmaker noted that both the sunflower and its discoverer thrived in "remote and hard-to-get-at areas of the West." Both were tough, tenacious specimens.

Yellow Mock Aster, *Eastwoodia elegans*

A small shrub found on the hot, dry hillsides of the southern and western San Joaquin Valley in California. The flowers of this member of the Sunflower Family grow in tight heads with no rays.

Eastwoodia elegans

Wilhelm Suksdorf

Mount Adams in southern Washington, one of the majestic
volcanic peaks of the Cascade Range, was the personal collecting
paradise of Wilhelm Suksdorf. Trekking along with his pack horse,
this retiring plant lover spent his days exploring the beauties of
mountain meadows, venturing into luminous ice caves, and climbing
up ice fields to the volcano's 12,276-foot-high summit.

Suksdorf's family thought of Wilhelm as a "child of nature." He
never married, living most of his life at home with his parents or
with one or another brother in White Salmon, Washington, a small
town along the Columbia River. Over time, Suksdorf's collection of
specimens grew large enough to crowd out any normal household.
When Wilhelm was sixty, he and a brother built a three-room house
for themselves, along with a separate herbarium to house the
collector's thousands of plants.

Suksdorf was never happier than when off by himself collecting.
He is said to have literally crawled over some of his collecting sites
in his endless search for new and interesting plants. To make ends
meet, the indefatigable collector sold plants that he had either
found or propagated in his garden. For half a century, he remained
instrumental in providing plants of the Pacific Northwest to the
rest of the world. One of his loveliest discoveries was *Suksdorfia
violacea,* a member of the Saxifrage Family named by Asa Gray for
his western correspondent.

Suksdorf did manage to make two extended forays to populated
places away from home. As a young man, he spent two years at the
University of California at Berkeley. Then later, when he was thirty-
six, a fond sister-in-law wrote an unsolicited letter to Asa Gray,
asking if a place "near the center of scientific culture" could be
found for Wilhelm. The shy bachelor must have been mortified.

Gray wrote back offering Suksdorf a position as his assistant. The
collector modestly declined, saying, "I am pretty sure that a
sedentary or indoor life would not agree with my health very well."
But with a second urging by Gray, Suksdorf went to Harvard. He
stayed for two years, until the death of Professor Gray. After that,
academic politics, along with his deep sense of loss for his mentor,
made him eager to return to the quiet of his open spaces.

Suksdorf ended his time on earth when he was eighty-two, the
victim of a strange accident. While off by himself in an uninhabited
area, he attempted to flag down a train. Unfortunately, he was all
but crippled by rheumatism and was unable to get out of the way of
the oncoming locomotive in time. Fortunately, before his death, he
had willed his collection of more than thirty thousand specimens to

Washington State University. There they remain as a fitting legacy of this shy but prolific collector.

Suksdorfia, *Suksdorfia violacea*

A slender perennial herb in the Saxifrage Family with a cluster of kidney-shaped, slightly lobed leaves growing on long stems from the bulblet-bearing root. Five-petaled violet flowers appear on a 4- to 12-inch wand from April to June. Found among rocks near small streams, from British Columbia to northwestern Oregon and east into northern Idaho and northwestern Montana.

Suksdorfia violacea

The Jones family c. 1903. Marcus, Mabel, Anna, Howard

Marcus Jones
1852–1934

The Jones' Popcorn Flower is a fitting tribute to Marcus Jones, a brilliant collector whose varied activities and caustic comments often exploded without regard for the consequences. Throughout his long life, Jones seemed to thrive on conflict and controversy.

Graduating Phi Beta Kappa from Grinnell College with degrees in languages and classics did not prepare Jones for the many directions his life took. After college, he moved to Salt Lake City, where, for two decades, he worked as a private explorer for the owner of the Denver and Rio Grande Railroad. During these years, Jones tutored himself in geology and botany and made scores of collecting trips into Mexico, Baja California, British Columbia, and the western states.

Given Jones's love of both nature and controversy, it was all but inevitable that he would be drawn into the legal battles being waged a century ago against the pollution generated by giant smelter operations in Utah and Montana. He purchased chemicals and test tubes and taught himself chemistry so he could serve as an expert witness in pollution court cases. This was hardly a remunerative career. In order to pay the bills, Jones's loyal and equally brilliant wife worked as a teacher and helped sell her husband's photographs and botanical specimens.

With characteristic forthrightness, Jones jumped into the national fray about who should be naming the plants of the West. He, along with several better-known California botanists, believed that western botanists had every right to describe and name the new plants they discovered. Eastern botanists resisted this claim and pressured their western colleagues to have all new names "cleared" by Asa Gray and his associates. Jones's strongly held views so antagonized the eastern establishment that he found himself cut off from the normal channels of debate in botanical journals.

Jones's response to this exclusion was to embark on an adventure in self-publishing. He purchased a printing press and typeset and printed eighteen issues of his own journal, *Contributions to Western Botany*. The purpose of the new journal was to facilitate the free expression of ideas. In an early editorial, Jones wrote:

> *It goes without saying that everyone has a right to publish anything he sees fit, the same right others have to criticize whatever is published.*

The pages of *Contributions to Western Botany* were sprinkled with Jones's uncensored comments about contemporary botanists. He called one "a typical toady," while another, he said, "posed as a botanist." In a unique obituary note, he wrote that "a botanical crook . . . has gone and relieved us of his botanical drivel."

Jones was equally opinionated about collecting. He devoted several pages of his journal to the kinds of paper to use and to the importance of wearing tennis shoes in the field. Even so, he allowed that his ways might not be for everyone. He wrote:

> *Don't let anyone fool you by saying that any one way is the only way of doing things. Use your own horse-sense. If you can make good specimens standing on your head dragging heavy boots, then do it. Results are what counts.*

Ironically, Jones himself sometimes fell short in the results department. He began, but never completed, a comprehensive flora of his favorite region, the Great Basin, or as Jones called it, the "Great Plateau." And despite his extensive knowledge of plants, Jones's voluminous writings were sometimes careless and, at times, downright wrong.

This irascible old codger spent his last years at Pomona College, to which he donated his extensive collection of some 100,000 specimens. Even at the age of eighty, he still played tennis with the students. His colleague Joseph Ewan remembered that although Jones returned "very hot from the sport, his frayed and not-a-little-dirty clothes in disarray, he stepped into the herbarium workroom gay and eager."

A year later, Jones met his death in characteristic style. He was returning from a field trip in the San Bernardino Mountains with the Parish Botanical Club, when he and his ancient Model T Ford were involved in a fatal accident. No doubt Jones was wearing his usual collecting outfit, "a black suit, vest and all, and a brown woolly cap with a large visor and looking still larger because within it was a bath sponge, larger than a baseball, to absorb the perspiration from his bald head." When it came to collecting, style meant nothing to Jones. As he had said before, "Results are what counts."

Jones' Popcorn Flower, *Plagiobothrys Jonesii*

A very bristly, erect plant with small white flowers. This member of the Borage Family is found in the mountains of California's Mojave Desert and east into Arizona and Utah, often growing with Creosote Bushes.

Plagiobothrys Jonesii

C. Hart Merriam

C. Hart Merriam
1855–1942

Florence Merriam Bailey
1863–1948

Lest we forget that there are naturalists other than botanists, consider the story of a brother and sister best known for their studies of mammals and birds, but for whom flowers also have been named.

C. Hart Merriam and his younger sister, Florence, grew up in upstate New York in an extended family that actively supported their interests. Their Aunt Helen, a trained botanist and plant collector, encouraged both children to learn about the natural world. Florence often tagged along with her brother as he began to trap animals and shoot birds, which he then embalmed or skinned. Their father encouraged these collecting activities by building a three-story museum near their home to house Hart's increasing number of animal specimens. (Perhaps their mother had outlawed the smelly, furry objects from her home!) Mr. Merriam again supported his son by underwriting the printing of Hart's first scientific work, *The Mammals of the Adirondack Region*.

After a short-lived career as a medical doctor, Hart followed his natural inclinations and obtained a position in the U.S. Department of Agriculture. Pleased with this opportunity to serve his country, he later wrote, "I felt that this might give me the long-cherished opportunity to establish a Biological Survey." Under his leadership, a systematic survey of the nation's biological resources was begun, and, within fifteen years, the number of listed mammals within the United States had nearly quadrupled. For such efforts, C. Hart Merriam is remembered as the father of American mammalogy.

Hart also evolved and popularized the concept of "life zones" or climatic belts housing different living things. As a child, he had read the German explorer Alexander von Humboldt's classic work on his travels through South America. Hart later recalled being

> *deeply impressed by Humboldt's account of animal and plant life in the lofty Andes, where the various species are grouped one above another in successive belts or zones according to differences of temperature and humidity.*

In 1889, Hart put together a small expedition to make the first comprehensive survey of the plants and animals of northern Arizona. He, his wife, and several colleagues hiked up the San Francisco Peaks, around the Painted Desert, and down into the Grand Canyon. Using changes in temperatures as his guide, Hart designated seven

Florence Merriam Bailey

life zones in this region—today called Desert, Pinyon-Juniper, Ponderosa Pine, Mixed Conifer, Spruce-Fir, Subalpine, and Alpine Tundra.

Florence Merriam adored her brother and wanted to follow in his every footstep. Though she had little formal education, Florence was able to enroll as a special student at Smith College. While in school, she became an environmental activist, entreating women to stop wearing feathers and even entire stuffed birds as millinery decorations. Florence also established an Audubon Society chapter at Smith, one of the nation's first.

Like her feathered friends, Florence migrated south after college, joining her brother in Washington, D.C. There, she married one of Hart's most talented collectors, Vernon Bailey. Bailey was a gentle pied piper, who often amazed the young by pulling a bat or lizard out of his pocket. For the next fifty years, the Baileys spent most summers conducting biological surveys in the mountains of Oregon or in the wilds of Texas and New Mexico.

To educate the public about the intriguing nature of birds, Florence began to write articles, such as "White-throated Swifts at Capistrano," which appeared in popular magazines. Her reputation grew with the publication of her *Handbook of Birds of the Western United States* in 1902. Replete with careful field observations and poetic prose, the handbook continued to be well received by amateur and professional birders for many years.

Both Florence and Hart were born into a family of naturalists, and both spent their lives studying and classifying the natural world. Florence's perceptive instructions for bird-watching are equally applicable to all nature study:

> *Four things only are necessary—a scrupulous conscience, unlimited patience, a notebook, and an opera-glass. The notebook enables one to put down the points which the opera-glass has brought within sight, and by means of which the bird may be found in the key; patience leads to trained ears and eyes, and conscience prevents hasty conclusions and doubtful records.*

Desert Poppy, *Arctomecon Merriamii*

A clump-forming plant growing on desert slopes in the Great Basin areas of southern Nevada and southeastern California. The mostly basal leaves have long, brown hairs. White flowers with six petals appear on tall, naked stems in April. Also known as the Bear Poppy.

Arctomecon
Merriami

Aven Nelson

Aven Nelson
1859–1952

The lark is up to meet the sun,
The bee is on the wing,
The ant his labors has begun,
The woods with music ring.

Shall bird and bee and ant be wise
While I my moments waste?
Oh, let me with the morning rise
And to my duties haste.

Aven Nelson, the son of Norwegian immigrants, took to heart these words from his McGuffey reader. Nelson pursued life with such energy and diligence that he became one of the best-known citizens of Wyoming. He achieved such prominence not as a politician but as an academic and the *alma pater* of Rocky Mountain botany.

Curiously, Nelson did not intend to be a scientist. He was the first to admit that he arrived at the fledgling University of Wyoming as a young man with a very different career path in mind:

> *I came to Wyoming expecting to teach English . . . but found myself slated for Biology, a field in which I had had no training, except a boy's unsatisfied curiosity in regard to the native flowers that grew in the ravines and on the clay hillsides of the open forest of oak and hickory [in Iowa].*

A strong desire to make his way in educational circles and the need to provide for his young wife gave Nelson his first impetus to study botany. Armed with two inadequate reference books, he began at the beginning, only to discover that "I had no conception of families, to say nothing of genera and species."

Nelson did, however, have a quick and retentive mind. The self-taught botanist soon became a consummate teacher. He conveyed enthusiasm for his subject, while always insisting on the importance of careful research. From the many letters written to him by appreciative students, Nelson emerges as a kindly and concerned father figure.

Nelson, his wife, Alice, and their two daughters spent many summers botanizing in the northern Rockies. In 1898, they collected in Yellowstone, the nation's first national park. When Nelson set to work naming the plants brought back from this trip, he was drawn into the sometimes vitriolic controversy then raging about how a plant should be named and who should do the naming. A conservative botanist at Harvard peppered him with criticisms about the inappropriateness of a name like "Yellowstonensis" and about his tendency to be a "splitter" by breaking his specimens down into more and more distinct species. In time, both Nelson and his critics moderated their views.

Nelson's long teaching career bridged the end of the Asa Gray era of plant classification and the beginning of modern botany with its emphasis on basic research into plant physiology, genetics, and ecology. Along with teaching, he found time to take on other responsibilities, from lay leadership in the Methodist Church to the presidency of the Botanical Society of America.

At the University of Wyoming, Nelson is remembered as the professor who selflessly took over as acting president and shepherded the small school through the difficult days of World War I. He also is honored for his work as curator of the school's herbarium. Working within a tiny budget, Nelson nurtured the herbarium into prominence by trading duplicate specimens with botanists and institutions around the country. He remained head of the herbarium until he retired at the age of eighty.

Family was important to both Aven and Alice Nelson. When their daughter, Neva, lost her husband, they welcomed her and her three young children back into their home. After the death of Alice in 1929, Nelson met and fell in love with Ruth Ashton, a graduate student half his age. She returned his feelings, and the two disappeared to Santa Fe, where they were married. At first, there was the expected flurry of raised eyebrows. But acceptance came soon, as friends and associates saw the deep affection and shared joy in plant collecting that bound this unlikely couple together.

Nelson's Delphinium, *Delphinium Nelsoni*

An erect perennial with few leaves. Bluish purple flowers with half-inch-long spurs bloom on simple stems up to 2 feet tall in May and June. Grows on dry plains from South Dakota west to Idaho and south to Colorado, New Mexico, Arizona, and Nevada.

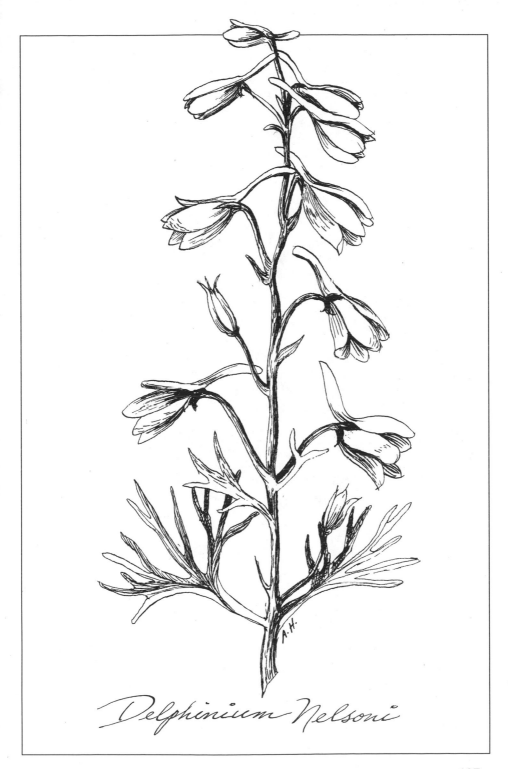

Delphinium Nelsoni

Agnes and Percy Train, with plant presses drying on the radiator.

Percy Train
1876–1942

Agnes Scott Train
1905–1991

What a pleasure it must have been to receive a Christmas letter from Percy and Agnes Train recounting their collecting adventures in the wilds of Nevada. In their letter of 1940, for example, Percy and Agnes report that they got an early start on the plant-collecting season. Spring was delectable in the high desert that year. "On the tablelands ranged great bands of sheep getting fat on tall green grasses."

The Trains set out on their collecting trip in a half-ton truck loaded with enough gear to survive for seven months, leaving barely enough room for their cocker spaniel. Behind the truck bounced a trailer. No campground for the Trains. "You haul in your supplies, establish camp near a spring or creek if you can, and carry on your work," they wrote. As pleasant as such a getaway might sound, all was not fun and games.

> To our sorrow we discovered why folks are in such a hurry to get away from the stagnant marshes. For a week we collected beautiful flowers in the hills, as bundled up in mosquito netting as tho we were plant hunting in South American jungles. When the wind blew toward the salt flats, we came out to breathe— when the wind blew OFF the flats, we hastily covered up, for great clouds of gnats, flies, and mosquitoes drifted in, eager to find their pound of flesh.

Percy Train spent most of his life in the desert. After studying at the Montana School of Mines, he rode to Nevada on horseback in 1905 to become an assayer. His interest in rocks led to his collecting fossils, which he found museums around the country were happy to purchase. Better yet, collecting kept him out in his beloved desert. Train was no city boy. He once stated emphatically, "Whenever I would hear water running from the tap I just wanted to scream."

Agnes Scott came to Nevada in 1928, leaving behind a job as a librarian in Chicago to marry Percy Train, a stocky fossil-hunter twice her age. With his usual flair, Percy arranged for the wedding to take place atop Lone Mountain, overlooking the ranching community of Lovelock. Their unlikely union joined together her research and recording skills with his desert survival know-how and buoyant enthusiasm.

A few years after their marriage, the Trains found themselves caught in the slumps of the Great Depression. Museums had no budgets to purchase their quality fossils. Upon hearing that money could be made collecting plants, Percy whistled and exclaimed, "I'll be damned. You mean to say colleges back East will pay for a dried specimen of *sagebrush, shadscale,* or *greasewood* flattened out by that two-bit slat press?"

The couple learned how to collect and press plants and began to travel with particular collecting themes in mind. On one trip, they explored the route of Clarence King's survey party, and on another, they combed Nevada for "alkali drought-resistant plants."

Word got back to Washington that the Trains were the right folks to carry out research for the Department of Agriculture on a project to record the medicinal uses of plants among the Shoshone and Paiute. Agnes wrote of their research efforts:

> *Big jolly Percy with his patience, hearty laugh, and plenty of cigarettes was a favorite with the squaws. One day we were having a particularly hard time of it, every plant remedy was simply, "You make a boiling—you drinking—he no hurt." After weeks of listening to the virtues of boiled roots, ground up chuckwallas, doses of skunk oil, and ant pudding, one begins to wonder how any are left alive to tell the tale.*

The "white-man-who-asked-questions" and the "one-with-the-pencil" were perfectly suited to the task of dredging up and carefully recording ancient Indian plant lore. Their research uncovered several useful plants. They identified an herb that produces a powerful birth-control agent and a root that yields a liquid to ease coughs. The Trains' most significant find was a creosote bush that produces an acid useful for preserving foods. This preservative became a secret weapon in World War II, when it was used to prevent spoilage of foods shipped to troops in hot climates. It must have been heartening for the Trains to discover that a pair of desert rats like themselves could have an impact on the wider world.

Arbutus Traini
Fossilized madrone leaf found by the Trains

Acer Scottiae
Fossilized maple leaf collected by the Trains

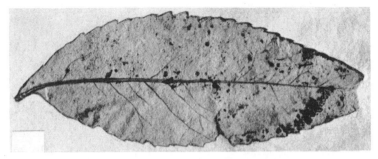

Arbutus Traini

Acer Scottiae

Edith Scamman with her Dodge touring car

Edith Scamman
1882–1967

Who would guess from looking at an old photo of Edith Scamman that the perky little lady with the straw hat perched on her head standing beside a 1928 Dodge touring car was, in reality, a fiercely independent flower and fern collector? Scamman's colleagues at Harvard's Gray Herbarium remember with nostalgia the botanist and her stories of collecting adventures.

Scamman's career as an intrepid collector did not begin until well after her fiftieth birthday. Still, she was descended from a long line of adventurous souls. In 1690, her colonial forebears were captured by Indians. Escaping a year later, they made their way back to their home, where they found a pitcher of beer still on the table as they had left it. An only child of older parents, Edith gained her love of adventure from her father, a restless man who spent his time pioneering in California while his womenfolk remained in Saco, Maine. Mr. Scamman once said of Maine, "It's a good place to be born, to get married, and to die." And he did just that.

Edith left Saco to attend college at Wellesley and then at Radcliffe, where she earned a master's degree in Middle English literature in 1909. After graduation, she returned home to care for her mother. In her spare time, Edith began teaching nature classes to children. Later in life, she was pleased to reveal that the actress Bette Davis had been one of her students. Edith's mother was much more comfortable when her daughter took on more traditional roles within the women's group of the Congregational Church.

Scamman's life changed dramatically with the death of her mother. In 1929, at the age of fifty-three, Edith drove her precious Dodge touring car down to Cambridge, rented a room near Radcliffe, and began to take botany classes. Thus began a thirty-year career as a collector and research associate at the Gray Herbarium.

During her new botanical career, Scamman made extensive collecting trips to Alaska, Iceland, Switzerland, and Latin America. Self-effacing and unpretentious, she loved roughing it: The more primitive the setting and the more problems to make life interesting, the better she seemed to like it. Scamman returned from her trips with tales to tell and with five thousand specimens, among them three Alaskan plants that were later named for her.

Scamman had a special love for Alaska, which she visited nine times. There, she would hire Eskimo guides or bush pilots to drop her off in areas of unglaciated starkness, with the simple request that they come back for her "later." Scamman once served as a barmaid in a Circle, Alaska, roadhouse to help out the owners, who were busy preparing meals for an onslaught of hungry hunters. In another remote village, she met Thomas Dewey, who was taking a break from his campaign for president. Scamman pulled back her parka hood, introduced herself to the Republican presidential hopeful, and said, "We're nearly neighbors, you from New York and me from Maine." The surprised Dewey replied, "My God, woman, what are you doing here?"

Scamman's lifelong interest was ferns. As a young woman, she wrote of her search for ferns around Saco: "When the list in my pine-lot had reached sixteen, I climbed my neighbors' fences and wandered farther afield." She later introduced a paper on ferns with these words:

> *As one studies the beautiful specimens gathered and preserved with so much care and reads the handwriting of many old labels of former years one can picture the delight and sense of achievement which came to many early fern students.*

Scamman was obviously smitten, both emotionally and intellectually, by botany; and her love of collecting turned her later years into productive pleasure. At a time when many of her friends were moving south to retire under palm trees, Scamman headed to the tropics to look for plants, making four collecting trips to Costa Rica.

Even though some might find the Alaskan flowers named for Edith Scamman a splendid tribute to her contributions, one wonders whether she would have felt more honored by the dozen or so children of Alaskan and Indian parentage named Edith after her. These namesake children are reminders of Scamman's friendship with native Alaskans, who came to appreciate the warm heart of this adventurous New England spinster.

Spring Beauty, *Claytonia Scammaniana*

A loose, clump-forming member of the Purslane Family with fleshy basal leaves. Blooms with one to two deep purple flowers per stem, each stem with two opposite leaves near the flowers. Found on stony slopes and screes up to 6,000 feet in the Alaska Range.

Claytonia Scammaniana

Mary DeDecker

Mary DeDecker
1909–

To Los Angelenos speeding north on the two-lane highway that leads them to vacation lands along the eastern Sierra Nevada, Independence, California, is not much more than a gas stop. How many of these passersby know that Independence is the home of the well-known botanist Mary DeDecker? And how many share her enchantment with the stark view to the south and east of Independence—range after range of treeless, brown mountains that fade into the arid expanses of the Mojave Desert and Death Valley?

When Mary DeDecker began married life with her husband, Paul, in the early 1930s, she had hopes of finishing college at UCLA. Paul, however, needed their only car for his job with the Los Angeles Department of Water and Power (DWP). This was during the Great Depression, when, as Mary remembers, "jobs were precious." But without transportation, Mary was unable to finish her degree.

In 1935, Paul was transferred by the DWP to its Owens Valley headquarters in Independence, where he remained until his retirement. Mary, besides caring for their two small girls, began to learn all she could about the native flowers of the region. This was a difficult task because there were no reference works on the plants of the eastern Sierra.

Over time, with the help of botanists John Thomas Howell and Philip Munz, both of whom DeDecker credits with strong guidance, the curious amateur became a respected authority on the flora of the eastern Sierra. She presently maintains a private herbarium of more than 6,400 specimens. During her many years of collecting, she has discovered five new species—one of which is named for her—and has been the first to identify several other species not previously known to grow in California.

In 1976, DeDecker found a new plant genus, *Dedeckera eurekensis,* near the undulating Eureka Dunes made famous by the sensuous photographs of Brett Weston. The drive from Independence to these sand mountains takes two hours, mostly on dusty gravel roads. In the Last Chance Mountains, near the southeast corner of Eureka Valley, the collector walked up a canyon, where she found a strange shrub that resembles buckwheat blooming on the sides of steep dolomite cliffs. Later, this site was named Dedeckera Canyon after this interesting plant. (Landforms cannot be named for living people, as can plants.)

When DeDecker first encountered the *Dedeckera eurekensis,* it was June and its buds had yet to open. She returned on July 4, a very hot time of year when few people would relish a hike in the desert, hoping to find the buds in bloom and possibly going to seed. DeDecker was met by a profusion of yellow blossoms on shrubs up to three feet high. "It was just golden," she recalls. "All over the dark cliffs, these golden bunches of this shrub."

The new plant was a puzzle, not to be found in any California flora. Thinking it was a new species of buckwheat, DeDecker sent specimens to the experts. Word came back that she had found a plant not known to science—the first new genus discovered in California in a quarter of a century.

DeDecker's interest in desert plants prompted her to begin a campaign to preserve the Eureka Dunes. In one of nature's wonders, these sand mountains capture the tiniest quantities of water. The water then trickles down to the base of the dunes, where it nourishes rare desert plants. These plants, however, were in danger of being destroyed by off-road vehicles. "It was terribly frustrating," she wrote. "I was sick as I went out and watched them tear up the place, spinning out the plants and seedlings, destroying animal habitats. . . . There's not another spot like it on the face of the Earth."

During the 1950s, the Bureau of Land Management (BLM) was struggling to come up with a desert-use plan that would pacify conservationists, off-road vehicle enthusiasts, miners, and stockmen. DeDecker threw herself into the debate, exhibiting unlimited patience and tenacity as she educated citizens, BLM staff, and politicians about the intrinsic value of desert lands. She went on to organize a letter-writing campaign on behalf of her beloved dunes.

The BLM finally bowed to public pressure in 1977 and closed the Eureka Dunes to motorized vehicles, a restriction at first blithely ignored by off-roaders, who put pleasure above protection. Today, the area is patrolled and the dunes exist in relative peace and quiet. In the nearby Last Chance Mountains, the tenacious *Dedeckera* blooms in midsummer, its yellow flowers a reminder of the self-taught botanist and lobbyist, who has done her part to preserve nature's beauty and diversity.

July Gold, *Dedeckera eurekensis*

A seldom-found shrub, which, because it blooms when the desert is so hot, is also seldom seen in flower. The tiny, bright yellow flowers have six spreading tepals (petallike parts) and bloom in small clusters. This member of the Buckwheat Family is found from 4,000 to 6,800 feet at the south end of the Last Chance Mountains in Death Valley and in the mountains bordering the nearby Saline Valley.

Dedeckera
eurekensis

Carl Sharsmith, 1938

Carl Sharsmith
1903–

A documentary film titled *Yosemite: The Fate of Heaven* ends with the image of an octogenarian in a National Park Service uniform sinking to his knees in a mountain meadow to examine a tiny flower. To thousands of campers, hikers, and plant lovers, this scene portrays the pied piper qualities of Carl Sharsmith, a naturalist who has been living and teaching in the High Sierra for more than sixty years. During those years, Sharsmith has explored nearly every nook and cranny of this land above the trees. And, he has probably come to understand the relationships among living things and the land more thoroughly than anyone has since John Muir.

Sharsmith's parents were Swiss, but Carl, first known as Karl Wilhelm Schaarschmidt, was born in the United States. In his father's restless search for the perfect chef's job, the family moved from New York to restaurants and resorts in Switzerland, London, Canada, Oregon, Utah, Texas, and California. Carl was a sensitive boy, often hiking alone with a knapsack his mother made for him, longing to know the names of the plants he saw on his wanderings.

Sharsmith quit school at fourteen to find work in lumber camps and on railroad crews. In his free moments, he filled journals with quotations from Shakespeare and the classics, notes about woodcraft and nature, and melodic passages from grand opera. These writings were to become an integral part of his mountain philosophy.

As Sharsmith matured, he was pulled in two directions. On the one hand, his love of nature and the freedom he felt out-of-doors led him to follow the advice of John Muir: "Climb the mountains and get their glad tidings." He found work piloting a group of boys known as the Trailfinders around the Sierra Nevada and the Indian Southwest. Later, he became a naturalist for the National Park Service in Yosemite. On the other hand, Sharsmith also felt a strong desire to continue his education. At the age of nineteen, he went back to junior high school. Twenty years later, he received a doctorate degree from the University of California.

After trying to feel at home teaching at the University of Minnesota and at Washington State College, Sharsmith returned to California and took a job at San Jose State University. The location was right. He could drive his 1935 Ford roadster from San Jose to Yosemite in less than a day. At San Jose State, Sharsmith amassed a substantial herbarium. His specialty was the study of alpine plants in the Sierra Nevada as compared to similar plants in Alaska, the Rocky Mountains, and Switzerland.

Some lives seem to follow an invisible path that leads to wisdom and to appreciation by their fellow humans. So it seems for Carl Sharsmith. He could hardly have realized at the time the effect on his thinking of his experiences in lumber camps as a penniless youth or the lasting importance of the leadership skills he gained with the Trailfinders. Pivotal to his career was his acceptance to the Yosemite School of Field Natural History, the model for interpretive training for the National Park Service. Much of his detailed scientific knowledge came from long backpacking trips with his botanist wife, Helen, in the years when few others were on the high-country trails. All these experiences shaped Sharsmith's skills as a premier interpreter of the plants, geology, and rhythms of the High Sierra. To the groups following Sharsmith on his guided hikes or listening to his campfire stories, he truly is the "mountain sage."

In 1991, Sharsmith was honored with the naming of *Draba Sharsmithii* by Dr. Reed Rollins of Harvard University, a botanist who first met Carl decades earlier when they were both doing research in the herbarium of Stanford University. This *Draba,* a member of the Mustard Family, had been discovered by Sharsmith high up on Lone Pine Creek in the eastern Sierra in 1937, and for years it had been given another name. The day he found the plant, Helen wrote in her journal about staying in camp while Carl climbed Mount Morrison. She had just finished washing clothes, developing film, and making plum cobbler for their dinner when Carl returned. "I'm so glad he is back," she wrote. "It was getting lonesome. He found a new Draba which seems very interesting."

Later, Carl and Helen separated. She moved on to the University of California at Berkeley, where she wrote *Flora of the Mount Hamilton Range of California*. Carl remains at San Jose State University, where he is an emeritus professor and curator of its herbarium. But like the plant that bears his name, Carl Sharsmith is most at home in the high mountain meadows, adapting to the vagaries of nature and anticipating the next season's summer sun.

Sharsmith's Draba, *Draba Sharsmithii*

The branches of this low, compact, much-branched, woody-based perennial are thick with tiny leaves. Three to ten tiny yellow blossoms appear on short, flowering stalks. Lance-shaped seed pods are twisted and curved. Grows in crevices and in sheltered granite areas of the southern and central Sierra Nevada, mainly on the eastern side at high elevations.

Draba
Sharsmithii

A. H.

143

Karen B. Nilsson

ABOUT THE AUTHOR

Karen Braucht Nilsson
1936–1991

"The sun is on the rock." As anyone who had the pleasure of
going on an outing with Karen Nilsson knows, that was her wake-up
call. For Karen, each new day was the beginning of an adventure.
With the coming of the sun, there were books to be read, mountains
to be climbed, and untold discoveries to be made.

With her humor, energy, and personal magnetism, Karen
drew people to herself and her activities. When with Karen, her
companions quickly learned that action was required and stillness
was sloth. Karen's intelligence was always at work, mining each
situation or organism she encountered for new ideas and insights,
creating universes within universes. The teacher in Karen could not
rest, but neither could the curious child. Sharing adventures with
this remarkable woman gave her companions the best of both.

Born in Oakland and raised in Merced, California, Karen
graduated from Stanford University with a degree in history. After
settling with her husband, Nils, on the San Francisco Peninsula,
she became active in a variety of civic, environmental, and cultural
groups, including the League of Women Voters, the Peninsula
Conservation Center, and TheatreWorks. Karen founded the
Environmental Volunteers, an organization that teaches hands-on
natural science to elementary schoolchildren throughout the San
Francisco Peninsula. She also served as codirector of the Trust for
Hidden Villa, a 1,600-acre environmental preserve in Los Altos Hills.

Amidst all this activity, Karen found time to become a writer and
publisher. Her Tioga Publishing Company produced works ranging
from handsome coffee-table books of photographs to small, elegant
volumes of poetry. All of Tioga's titles, however, reflected Karen's
abiding interest in the people, history, and natural environment of
California and the West. Several of her publications received regional
and national book awards.

This book was Karen's last publishing project. She began the
research for it to satisfy her own curiosity. And to whet yours, she
decided to write about the people she discovered while poking
about in herbariums and arboretums. The underlying message in
this, as in all Karen's work, is this: Expand your universe through
your own curiosity. Riches beyond measure can be found under a
rock, inside a flower, or within the pages of a book.

ABOUT THE BOOK

Karen Nilsson had not quite completed the manuscript for *A Wild Flower by Any Other Name* before her untimely death from cancer in 1991. In the months that followed, her husband, Nils, and a group of friends undertook the challenge of realizing her vision. The book you hold in your hands is our collective memorial to this warm, engaging woman, who left a lasting imprint on those she touched.

Had Karen been with us, she would have enjoyed supervising this ad hoc publishing group. It was made up of people she knew and trusted. As we worked through problems, we often felt her red pen hovering over us. At times, our search for more information or for photographs led us to places we had never been. That would have pleased Karen enormously. In life, she had often been our catalyst, pushing us to venture into the unknown. And our catalyst she remains.

Acknowledgments

So many people have contributed to the research and publication of this book that it is impossible to acknowledge them all by name. Still, on behalf of Karen, we would like to thank the following individuals for their special contributions to this project:

Publication Committee	Additional Assistance
Linda Elkind	Barbara Bennigson
Diane Hart	Jean Cargill
Andrea Hendrick	Mabel Crittenden
Christy Holloway	Mary Hallesy
Kathy McFarland	Ellie Huggins
Nils Nilsson	Yvonne Jacobson
Lennie Roberts	Denise Stanford
Lynn Torin	The Environmental Volunteers

Special thanks also are due the following institutions, whose people gave so generously of their time and knowledge to Karen while she was researching this book:

Gray Herbarium at Harvard University

Hunt Institute for Botanical Documentation at Carnegie Mellon University

Missouri Botanical Garden

FURTHER EXPLORATIONS.

If this book has sparked your interest in native plants, you may wish to make some discoveries of your own. The following suggestions may help you with your explorations:

- Browse through field guides to wildflowers, plants, and trees in your local bookstore or library to learn more about indigenous plant species.

- Take a class in botany or ecology at your local college or university.

- Check the phone book for a listing of your state's native plant society and give that group a call.

- Visit a local botanical garden, arboretum, or natural history museum to observe labeled plants. Ask staff members and volunteers to suggest good areas for field studies of native plants.

- Get in touch with local garden clubs and conservation groups. Most have members who love to share their expertise and encourage explorations. Some may offer tours of botanically interesting sites.

- Contact the local office of a national conservation organization, such as the Audubon Society or Sierra Club, and ask for information about local activities and resources.

- Go on naturalist-led walks and tours when you visit local, state, and national parks.

- Write or call the National Wildflower Research Center and ask for their information package. The NWRC supports wildflower research, landscaping with native plants, and efforts to preserve America's wildflower heritage throughout the United States.

National Wildflower Research Center
2600 FM 973 North
Austin, TX 78725-4201
(512) 929-3600

SOURCES FOR
BOTANICAL NOMENCLATURE

The naming of plants remains an area of controversy, as old groupings and divisions are reexamined in the light of emerging genetic information. The plant names used throughout this book are based on the following sources:

Cronquist, Arthur, et al. *Intermountain Flora; Vascular Plants of the Intermountain West, USA*. 6 vols. New York: New York Botanical Gardens, Columbia University Press, 1977.

Hickman, James C., ed. *The Jepson Manual; Higher Plants of California*. Berkeley: University of California Press, 1993.

Kearney, Thomas H., et al. *Arizona Flora*. Berkeley: University of California Press, 1960.

Munz, Philip A., et al. *A California Flora*. Berkeley: Rancho Santa Ana Botanic Garden, University of California Press, 1959.

Rickett, Harold William. *Wild Flowers of the United States*. 7 vols. New York: New York Botanical Garden, McGraw-Hill Book Co., 1971.

PHOTO CREDITS

Page

NOTES